ABOUT THE MINISTRY

About the Ministry

JOHN STACEY

WIPF & STOCK · Eugene, Oregon

Wipf and Stock Publishers
199 W 8th Ave, Suite 3
Eugene, OR 97401

About the Ministry
By Stacey, John
Copyright©1967 Methodist Publishing - Epworth Press
ISBN 13: 978-1-5326-3511-3
Publication date 6/16/2017
Previously published by Epworth Press, 1967

Every effort has been made to trace the current copyright
owner of this publication but without success. If you have
any information or interest in the copyright,
please contact the publishers.

CONTENTS

ACKNOWLEDGEMENTS	6
1 OUR PREDICAMENT IN THE MINISTRY	7
2 THE NATURE OF THE MINISTRY	38
3 THE MINISTRY TODAY	73
APPENDIX I	107
APPENDIX II	109
APPENDIX III	111

ACKNOWLEDGEMENTS

THE seminal ideas for this book emerged from discussions in the years 1964-5 with my friends Raymond Billington, George Lockett, David Stacey and Gordon Wakefield. I am grateful to them, but for the opinions now expressed I must accept entire responsibility. My debt to my brother, the Rev. David Stacey of Wesley College, Bristol, who has constantly placed his theological expertise at my disposal, is considerable, and I gratefully acknowledge it. The Rev. Rupert Davies, also of Wesley College, made some valuable suggestions. I should also like to record my gratitude to Miss Mary Briant who typed the manuscript and to Miss Audrey Goodburn who read the proofs.

I am grateful to the Edinburgh House Press for the quotation from *New Forms of Ministry*, edited by David Paton, which they published in London, 1965. Also to the SCM Press for use of Anthony T. Hanson's *The Pioneer Ministry*.

John Stacey,
Hoylake,
Cheshire.
1967.

Chapter I

OUR PREDICAMENT IN THE MINISTRY

The Methodist ministry has a creditable record of devoted service for the Kingdom of God. Its effectiveness in building up the life of the Church through preaching and administration of the sacraments has for many years been self-evident. As the Anglicans acknowledged in the Interim Statement of 1958, 'The exercise of this ministry by those ordained in the Methodist Church has been manifestly owned and used by God for his glory in converting sinners and perfecting saints, through the proclamation of the gospel and the use of sacramental means of grace.'[1] Its pastoral practice and its administration of the churches has generally been of a high order. The itinerant system, the universal loyalty to the 'connexion', the endemic friendliness of Methodists and not least the financial equality have made it a band of brothers. The grateful acknowledgement of such facts is necessary to ensure that in facing our predicament the iron is not allowed to enter the soul. It is in no carping spirit that we must examine the situation in which the Methodist ministry finds itself today.

The shortage of candidates for the Methodist ministry worries everyone who cares for the health of the Church. As most Methodists will have heard *ad nauseam*, in 1965 the Home Mission Report[2] emerged from its customary euphoria to lay the facts before us. In 1955, one hundred and twenty-four candidates were accepted for the ministry, but a decline followed until in 1964 there were eighty-nine, in 1965 only fifty-five. In 1966 there were only fifty. If this fall in the number of candidates accepted was due to the application of a more rigorous standard to a constant number of candidates, no one would imagine that Methodism had gone into decline, though there might be mild complaints from officials who know that the Church needs an intake of one hundred to a hundred-and-twenty men each year to replace losses due to death, retirement, and resignation. But the opposite is the case. It is the number of men offering for the ministry that causes alarm. The following table makes the situation clear.

Year	Number sent forward by Synods	Number accepted by the Conference
1956	144 1 Senior	110 0 Senior
1957	149 5 ,,	114 3 ,,
1958	148 1 ,,	116 0 ,,
1959	125 1 ,,	99 0 ,,
1960	103 3 ,,	82 2 ,,
1961	97 3 ,,	84 2 ,,
1962	98 3 ,,	86 3 ,,
1963	103 4 ,,	90 2 ,,
1964	105 3 ,,	89 1 ,,
1965	67 2 ,,	55 0 ,,
1966	59 3 ,,	50 2 ,,
1967	55 5 ,,	49 4 ,,

It is to the credit of those who serve upon the Connexional Candidates Examination ('July') Committee that they have not allowed these figures to stampede them into a drastic lowering of standards. The percentage of candidates accepted from those sent forward by Synods over these years works out as follows (to the nearest $\frac{1}{2}$%): 1956, $76\frac{1}{2}$%; 1957, $76\frac{1}{2}$%; 1958, $78\frac{1}{2}$%; 1959, 79%; 1960, $79\frac{1}{2}$%; 1961, $86\frac{1}{2}$%; 1962, 88%; 1963, $87\frac{1}{2}$%; 1964, 85%; 1965, 82%; 1966, 85%; 1967, 89%. Unless during the last five years there has been a general improvement in the quality of the candidates one must conclude that there has been a slight lowering of standards.

The decline in the number of candidates has to be set against the background of the decline in the number of local (lay) preachers for, under present regulations, a man must normally be a fully accredited local preacher before he can offer for the ministry. In 1933 we had 35,000 local preachers. We now have 22,000. Well over one third have been lost since 1932. And the situation grows worse. In the calendar year of 1965 the loss of 'preachers on trial' was nearly one eighth. New recruits dropped by nearly two hundred—five hundred and thirty-eight instead of seven hundred and twenty-seven the previous year, and sixty were lost in transfer from one circuit to another. To quote the Secretary of the Local Preachers' Department, the Rev. David Francis: 'During the year more than three hundred preachers on trial either themselves withdrew from training or were withdrawn as unsuitable.' In 1966 the numbers were similar. Figures like these make the prospect of a rise in the number of men offering for the ministry unlikely.

These figures have in turn to be set against the background of a declining Church membership. Most Methodists know the situation only too well. In 1932 there were eight hundred and fifty-six thousand Methodist members and in 1966 six hundred and ninety thousand (figures to the nearest thousand), a loss of over one sixth in thirty-four years. The Home Mission Report to which reference has already been made states clearly the bleak prospect: 'The rate of decline is increasing, and we must face the unpalatable fact that if the present trends continue we may lose another hundred thousand members by 1975.'

There are some factors common to these declines that are only too obvious. They are the subjects of expatiation in countless sermons. Agnosticism has become fashionable, and if people don't openly embrace it they are inevitably affected by its prevalance. Religious habits tend to lose what sanction they had. Young people are confirmed and received into membership of their local church; they go away to college or university, but, in spite of the excellent work of college chaplains and university Methodist Societies, some are affected by the prevailing mood of doubt and their links with the Church grow weaker and finally snap. In a different climate of opinion some of them might have offered for the ministry.

Affluence is another such factor. It seems clear that, when a man has reached the point of considering seriously whether to offer for the ministry or not, the prospect of life on a Methodist minister's stipend does not unduly deter him. When the Renewal Group in Methodism sent out questionnaires to those who attended conferences in 1964 and 1965 for those considering the possibility of offering for the ministry, they included a question: 'If you decided not to enter the ministry did any of the following considerations affect your decision?' Of these considerations, 'pay and prospects' was beaten into bottom place only by 'uncertainties about church union negotiations'. The danger of affluence, one supposes, is that, like agnosticism, it creates a climate of opinion in which it becomes less likely that the question of offering for the ministry will become a genuine option. With gracious living, fitted carpets, and yearly increments it needs strong conviction to face the possibility of life on the quarterly cheque from the circuit steward.

But the general religious and social state of the community must concern us less—because it is less germane to our theme—than the image of the ministry in the eyes of those who could conceivably offer themselves for it. In what ways does the Methodist ministry as it is today put them off? Here the Renewal Group questionnaires (eighty-seven replies from a hundred-and-forty sent out) again provide useful evidence. Though doubtless at these conferences the difficulties and problems of the ministry were squarely faced, it must be noted that the ministers who spoke were usually of the younger, more vigorous and more radical type. This is the testimony of the potential candidates themselves. 'I thought,' writes a teacher, 'that if men such as this could stay in then there was hope that I possibly could.' This fact makes their subsequent doubts the more depressing.

Many of these men thought that the typical Methodist minister was over-burdened with cumbersome and largely pointless administration. One student writes 'that they (ministers) should be the administrative prop of Methodism is wasting their time,' and another: 'talking to those present it was obvious that the ministry and the whole Church workings will have to be considerably and quickly modernized.' But the complaint goes beyond the mere amount of administration. It is the introverted nature of so much of the minister's work that is criticized. As a teacher puts it, 'It seems to me that the Church is tied up as an institution and that the minister has to dabble around as a kind of Jack-of-all-trades, always tied up with the faithful.' This way of life, complains another, 'is responsible for ministers becoming out of touch with non-Christians.' 'Ministers generally spend far too much time looking after their own sheep,' writes an Education Committee clerk. And presumably the more books and articles that are written criticizing the present patterns of ministerial life, and the more avidly they are read by our thinking young men, the more acute will become the shortage of candidates.

A further factor is that, for good or ill, the teaching on lay vocation which has been taught and preached so vigorously in the Church over the last decade is coming home to roost. If we tell people often enough that they can serve God as effectively (and even be *called* to do so) as bank clerks and probation officers as they can as ministers, then we ought not to be surprised if they take us at our word and become bank clerks and probation officers. This, we are constantly being told, is the day of the 'layman's Church'. The list of books written in the last year or two on the importance of the layman in the Church is formidable. Can we then complain if people wish to remain laymen? Why should they renounce the lay apostolate which is being clapped on the back for the ordained ministry which is having its nose rubbed in the dirt? Some of the Renewal Group replies confirm this. 'The alternative for me is teaching (I am a graduate in economics, about to enter an Education Department), and it seems to me that in this vocation I might have more chance to exercise the priesthood of the Christian.' 'Social work, which I am undertaking full-time from August, 1965, seems to offer more face-to-face relationships at depth.' 'I am training to be a teacher. In this field I hope to be as "effective" as the ordinary minister.' At least one of these conferences for interested young men did what the whole Church has been doing over recent years, for, says one young man, 'Such stress was laid upon the need for believing laymen, that I was convinced that this was my role.'

The Liturgical Movement has been a factor in this situation. If one sees the two aims of the Movement as a proper stress on the objectivity of the Word and Sacraments (which must be held together) as distinct from the experiences they can arouse and a proper insistence on the exercise in worship and evangelical activity of the corporate priesthood of the whole Church, then the second has furthered the concept of 'the layman's Church'. Laymen reading the Epistle and Gospel at Communion, bringing forward the elements to the table, saying the biddings in the intercessions and administering the wine, these are overt actions which express the truth that liturgy is not 'read prayers' but, as its derivation makes clear, the 'work of the people'. No one would question the value of this in the task of making the Church be the Church, and if it means, as it usually does (and not only in Protestantism), the end of clerical dominance and the view of the minister or priest as a miracle worker, that is all to the good. But if it gives any encouragement to the opinion that the minister is a mere functionary (a discussion of this is to follow), or that the priesthood of all believers means that a minister is no more than a full-time layman, then it is being taken too far. It is not our concern to criticize this emphasis on the laity, and certainly not to condemn it, but simply to raise at this stage the question whether or not in a 'layman's Church' a shortage of candidates for the ministry is not inevitable unless one has a more adequate doctrine of the ministry than, for example, the Methodist Deed of Union would allow.

We turn now to the losses from the Methodist ministry. In Methodist technical terms, 'withdrawal' means going out before ordination and 'resignation' going out afterwards. Both give cause for concern. In the winter of 1965 a Methodist theological student who had 'withdrawn' wrote an article in what purports to be an *avant-garde* Methodist magazine which he called 'I turned my collar back again'. The article recognized that the role of the minister in preaching and pastoral work demanded both authority and conviction, but confessed that, as for the writer, these were unobtainable in an age of theological confusion. It went on to complain that the minister occupied a largely irrelevant position on the periphery of modern life. But such explicitness and publicity are the opposite of the norm. Withdrawals are usually quiet affairs and the undertaking every ordinand gives that if he has to resign he will 'go out quietly' ensures that resignations are carried out with discretion. Every year names silently disappear from the Minutes of Conference—men sunk practically without trace. This, one would think, is a good system in so far as it saves the Church from that open scandal which from time to time embarrasses others, but it makes it extraordinarily difficult to know the true state of affairs. And that means the possibility of under-estimation, and complacency, or over-estimation, and panic. All we can attempt here is some rough guess based upon personal memories and calculations.

One man, for example, calculates that, of the hundred and fifty-two people he spent some time with in his theological college, twenty are now out of the ministry, a loss of 13% in the eighteen years since he left. Another recalls that, of the small company of eighteen who went back to open a theological college after the war, three are no longer Methodist ministers, a loss of nearly 17% in nineteen years. A slightly younger man knows that three out of thirty have gone in sixteen years, a 10% loss. Another man of the same year, going carefully through the list of all the men who were in college with him in 1950, discovers that, out of a total of seventy-six in that year, sixteen have left the ministry, a loss of 21% over the sixteen years. He points out that they are not all lost to the wider ministry of the Church, for at least four have become Anglican priests, one a Church of Scotland minister, one a Baptist minister, one has gone to the Billy Graham Organization and one to the Unevangelized Fields Faith Mission, and there may be others in other ministries (the secrecy makes it hard to be precise). But they have left the Methodist ministry. One does not have to be a statistician to draw broad conclusions from these samples. Just as the BBC television commentators with their 'swingometer' on the night of the General Election forecast the size of the Government majority from a handful of results, so we can see the approximate size of the trend of losses during the years which are covered by the samples, in these cases the years since the war.

Our chief consideration, however, cannot be with shortage of candidates nor with withdrawals and resignations, but must be with what is determinative for them both, the present state of the ministry. In what state is the Methodist ministry today? Can it truly be said that it is in a predicament? In the slightly mixed-up article already referred to, there is the assertion that 'in an age of theological confusion it is impossible to perform with conviction the traditional tasks of the ministry'. We turn then to the theological confusion.

If we allow two illustrations of it, the first must be the Doctrine of God. When in 1963 many working ministers found themselves, under the pressure of its publicity, working through the pages of *Honest to God,* they realized for the first time that theism as they had always understood it was being called in question. That an epistemological debate had been launched by Kant's *Critique of Pure Reason*; that, as John Kent points out[3], the materials for a Doctrine of God acceptable to Protestant Liberalism has been steadily eroded during the nineteenth century; that linguistic philosophers had for some years been putting large question marks over the traditional religious words; that Tillich's *The Shaking of the Foundations* had been published in England in 1949, Bonhoeffer's *Letters and Papers from Prison* in 1953 and Bultmann's *New Testament and Mythology* in the same year, these were facts that had registered only with those who were theologically wide awake. For the rest, and this inevitably included a high proportion of the older men, it was Robinson who opened the eyes. Men began to see what was happening to the familiar concepts and language that had been used of God. They started to read Tillich and discovered that their long accepted notion of 'God as a being, the highest being' who 'has brought the universe into being at a certain moment (five thousand or five billion years ago), governs it according to a plan, directs it toward an end, interferes with its ordinary processes in order to overcome resistance and to fulfil his purpose, and will bring it to consummation in a final catastrophe' is a concept that 'transforms the infinity of God into a finiteness which is merely an extension of finitude.'[4] Though it is true that in his exposition of the terms 'self-transcendent' and 'ecstatic', and in equating God with being itself rather than one being among others,*[5] Tillich points the way to faith, the reader has first to come to terms with the fact that the symbolic language which he has used for so long about God cannot be taken literally. He may well be, as Tillich admits, 'afraid to transcend the personalistic symbolism of the religious language.'[6] Contemplating the possibility of a 'God above the God of theism'[7], the 'God who is the ground of everything personal and as such is not *a* person'[8] may increase his confusion.

Or if the minister turned from Robinson to read Paul van Buren, whose book, *The Secular Meaning of the Gospel*, was also published in 1963, he did not find his doubts laid smoothly to rest. Van Buren, commenting upon the distinction between the Gospel (which 'proclaims God's act of grace reaching down to rescue man') and religion (which 'has to do with man reaching up to find or define God'), argues that modern secular man has a deeper problem than whether grace or legalism is the basis of God's relationships with men. To quote again the famous sentences, 'We do not know "what" God is, and we cannot understand how the word "God" is being used. . . . The problem of the Gospel in a secular age is a problem of the logic of its apparently meaningless language.'[9] When the reader comes to understand that the traditional language of the

* The God who is *a* being is transcended by the God who is Being itself, the ground and abyss of every being.[5]

supernatural has died 'the death of a thousand qualifications', his confusion is one from which the philosophical method of linguistic analysis has some difficulty in rescuing him.

There is no need to turn to other radical authors, for the result would be the same. No one would wish to deny the necessity, and indeed the inevitability, of the debate about God, nor the fact that for some it has increased and not diminished the viability of the Gospel. The point to be made here is that, when the busy minister, whose work will not allow him to read more than one book every other week, is plunged into it through, perhaps, the medium of *Honest to God*, then, unless he is able to respond with fundamentalist or Barthian dogmatism, he becomes confused.

The second illustration is to be found in the questioning of Christian origins. It is all very well to say, as Professor Anthony Hanson points out,[10] that what determines the image of God is an earthly life of thirty years, but if you are constantly being told that you cannot know anything certain about that earthly life, you find yourself with nothing left on which to build an image of God. What will remain to be preached about if the scepticism of the Form critics is carried much further? *Honest to God* might have introduced its reader to Bultmann as well as to Tillich. In his *Theology of the New Testament*[11] Bultmann argues that belief in the messiahship of Jesus arose with and out of belief in his resurrection. The confession at Caesarea Philippi is 'an Easter-story projected backward into Jesus' life-time, just like the story of the Transfiguration.'[12] 'The account of Jesus' baptism is legend, certain though it is that the legend started from the historical fact of Jesus' baptism by John. It is told in the interest, not of biography, but of faith.' 'The Temptation story, which involves reflection about what kind of a messiah Jesus was, or what kind of messiah the Christian believes in, is legend. The story of

Jesus' Entry into Jerusalem has been coloured by legend, and the passion-narrative is also to a considerable degree overspread with legend.' Obviously there is need here for a close definition of 'legend', but when a man who has been trained to believe that Christianity is a historical religion, rooted and grounded in the solid stuff of history, is abruptly confronted with the assertion that what actually happened is by no means the same as what is recorded as having happened, and for reasons that are cogently argued, he begins to have his doubts. Form criticism does not of course begin nor end with Bultmann and in case one is accused of beating some anti-academic drum it must be emphasized that much of the work of Form critics has been constructive and of inestimable value to the study of Christian origins. They have, as their name implies, studied and described the forms in which traditions about Jesus were handed down and they have related these traditions to the appropriate situations in the life of the early Church. Much of this is constructive work. Stephen Neill shows the balanced judgement we have come to expect from him when he says of the Form critics, 'But it is impossible that all the careful study they have directed to the Gospels should prove to be without value; and, provided that we keep certain critical reservations in mind, we are likely to find that they have much that is profitable to teach us.'[13] But the fact remains that, in an age where far more questions are asked than answers given, the destructive seems to compel attention with so much more ease than the constructive.

Some of the most radical questions that have been asked in the field of Christian origins are questions about the Resurrection. Ronald Gregor Smith in his book, *Secular Christianity*, may be taken as an example of the modern radical critic. He argues strongly for a heterodox view, starting from two presuppositions. One is a view of history which includes both 'the construction of the past which may be elicited by historical investigation' (*Historie*) and 'history in the sense that it connects with your own life' (*Geschichte*). The other is the 'eschatological reality of the life and death of Jesus' in which eschatology as an addendum on the last things is dismissed in favour of 'the message concerning Christ, that we in our present lives may be confronted by his reality in such a way that we may enter into a new life.' From these two presuppositions he moves forward to the view that the Resurrection is a reality in the sense that faith in 'the historical being of God for men in Christ' is expressed in the affirmation of the Risen Christ. Faith in the Christ who is apprehended historically and who confronts us, in judgement and with the offer of new life, eschatologically, is faith in the Risen Christ. 'The resurrection . . . is a way of affirming the forgiving purpose of God in the historical reality of the life of Christ.'[14] But this does not demand the orthodox view of the Resurrection. We must not fall for the 'immense and constant temptation at this point to elevate the legends of the empty tomb . . . into the separate status of objective "happenings".'[15] Then follows the sentence which has the orthodox howling for his blood: 'So far as historicity is concerned, *historische* fact, it is necessary to be plain: we may freely say that the bones of Jesus lie somewhere in Palestine.'[16] Methodism does not easily breed the kind of dogmatism which rejects the heterodox out of hand. But there is no denying the fact that in the consideration of the 'new' theology there is the possibility of confusion. After a man has read Gregor Smith is he to re-write all his Easter sermons or not?

Doubt has also been cast on Christian origins by some (a minority) scholars who have worked on the Dead Sea Scrolls. Edmund Wilson argued in *The Scrolls from the Dead Sea* for the non-uniqueness of Christianity, and although he believed that Dupont Somner overplayed his hand when he stated that the Teacher of Righteousness was in some respects an exact prototype of Jesus he believed that the 'martyr's career' of Jesus was prepared for him in this dissident branch of Judaism; that 'the ritual of the Last Supper ultimately derives from the sect'[17], and he made the astonishing statement that 'the monastery . . . between the bitter waters and precipitous cliffs . . . is, perhaps, more than Bethlehem or Nazareth, the cradle of Christianity.'[18]

Dr J. M. Allegro, a former Methodist theological student, has popularized the doubts which these views cast upon Christian origins. In his widely-read book, *The Dead Sea Scrolls,* he has drawn the parallels between the use of Scripture texts in the Scrolls and in the New Testament,[19] and pointed out the affinities, real and imaginary, between the Qumran Community and the Church,[20] and between their respective messianic conceptions. The uniqueness of Christianity is whittled away. Much is then made of the resemblance between the Qumran Sect and Jesus and the suggestion is offered that the prevalance of a 'Third Order' of the Essenes is 'a very possible means of access to Qumran ideas for Jesus.'[21] Although, as Millar Burrows points out, 'Christians should have no reluctance to recognize anticipations of Christianity in the Dead Sea Scrolls, or in other Jewish writings, if or when they really exist. The Gospel was given as the fulfilment of what was already revealed',[22] and although the extremism of Dupont Somner and the radical views of Dr Allegro, as popularized by him in a number of television programmes, have been duly balanced by more conservative opinion,* there remains the impression

---

* 'For myself I must . . . confess that, after studying the Dead Sea Scrolls for seven years, I do not find my understanding of the New Testament substantially affected.'[23] There is an excellent paragraph on the uniqueness of Christianity at the end of *The Ancient Library of Qumran and Modern Biblical Studies* (p. 184) by Frank Moore Cross Jr. See also chapter 3 of *The Zadokite Fragment and the Dead Sea Scrolls,* H. H. Rowley, 1952; Part II of Millar Burrows' *More Light on the Dead Sea Scrolls,* 1958; chapter 6 of R. K. Harrison's *The Dead*

that the historical foundations of the Christian faith are perhaps not quite as secure as they were thought to have been.

The debate on the Doctrine of God and the questioning of Christian origins are two examples to illustrate the general theological ferment of our times. The truth is that wherever one turns in the theological field, to the Doctrine of Creation, to Christology, to the Atonement, to the Resurrection, to Eschatology, or to the Doctrine of the Church, one finds a prevalence of searching, radical questions and a dearth of satisfactory answers. And the busy minister, whose timetable cannot be made to include a thorough theological enquiry, may well find himself not a little confused.

The changes that have taken place, and are taking place in moral theology have not exactly helped to stabilize the situation. They are closely linked to it, for confusion about the nature of God and the historicity of Christ inevitably causes questions to be asked in the field where 'the will of God' and 'the teaching of Jesus' have been so determinative—that is, the moral field. Again, if the kind of reader we are thinking of used *Honest to God* as his source book, he will have met the 'new morality', and he will have understood that in it the notion that 'certain things are always "wrong" and "nothing can make them right" '[24] is abandoned in favour of an ethic based on the dictates of love in any given situation. The only intrinsic evil now is the lack of love. Absolutist ethics are out. The controversial Report of the Working Party to the British Council of Churches in 1966, *Sex and Morality*, describes the position which 'regards moral rules as possessing permanent and absolute validity, so that the morality of a

---

Sea Scrolls, 1961—where the writing off of the uniqueness of Christianity is shown to be a case of *post hoc ergo propter hoc;* and much other literature.

particular act is ultimately determined by whether or not it falls under the relevant rule' as 'the extreme conservative position' and states that the working party finds this position 'untenable'. H. A. Williams in his essay, *'Theology and Self-awareness'* in *Soundings*, gives illustrations of a more 'situational' approach. In war, for one man to love is 'to steel himself to the task of systematic killing',[26] but for another it is to refuse to kill. 'Or', continues Williams, 'we can imagine circumstances when to steal would be a greater virtue than not to steal', and then follow those two illustrations of the rightness, in exceptional circumstances, of fornication, which brought down so much wrath upon his head.

There is no doubt but that the existence of the new morality has affected the pastoral work of the Methodist minister, particularly his work among the young. He may meet their questions about pre-marital sexual intercourse with a rigid defence of the traditional position or he may try to teach them that, in almost every conceivable situation, charity demands chastity. The relevant point is that new questions are being asked, and answers must be given. Adaptation rather than confusion is the appropriate word here.

Where confusion tends to creep in is in relation to those 'sins' which the minister has up till now eschewed on the basis of an absolutist ethic. If the whole notion of absolutism goes, then he is in trouble. As far as Methodists are concerned the 'social gospel' is the area where this is most clearly demonstrated. Total abstinence and pacifism will serve as examples. It is difficult to estimate the precise extent of the former in Methodism. Some two thirds of the Methodist ministry are, according to the last sociological survey, total abstainers, but the proportion of the laity is unknown. It varies considerably from area to area and, one would think, is less than that of the ministers. The statement in the *Manual of Membership* that 'most

Methodists' are total abstainers is open to question. Though there are some, like Kenneth Greet,[27] who argue cogently for total abstinence for what are essentially pragmatic reasons (that is to say, answering the 'new morality' question, 'What does love demand in this situation?'), the majority are total abstainers because they cherish the notion that 'the thing itself' is wrong. The question succeeds in generating far more emotion than it deserves (witness the fuss being made about the use of fermented wine in Holy Communion) and the staunch total abstainers in the Methodist ministry have a feeling, as they see younger ministers and laymen turn away from the absolutist position, that the ethical standards of the Church are being undermined.

The traditional pacifist position is in the same case, though the numbers concerned are lower. In the summer of 1963 the Methodist Peace Fellowship sent out a questionnaire on the Christian attitude to war to all Methodist ministers under the British Conference. It revealed that almost a thousand Methodist ministers held pacifist convictions (seven hundred of them are enrolled members of the Methodist Peace Fellowship). Like the total abstainers, the pacifists are divided between those who are trying to make pacifism viable in the present theological and ethical upheaval and those who are content to reiterate their absolutist position. For the latter there is 'a thing itself', be it war, or the taking of life, or violence, or force, which is wrong under all circumstances and as a matter of principle there could not, and do not, exist circumstances in which it could be right. For the former, R. J. Billington speaks when he says that 'the only possible absolute for the Christian is the absolute of love',[28] and then proceeds to make his case on that more pragmatic and 'situational' ground. This shift has caused uncertainty and confusion in some Methodist minds.

But for every hour the average Methodist minister spends reading about, and thinking through, theological and ethical questions he spends five (perhaps ten?) doing the work of the Church. What is the case here? Can he turn from his theological and ethical predicaments to find a deep conviction that his work in the Church is of profound significance and undisputed relevance?

Pastor Althausen of the Evangelical Church of Berlin-Brandenburg begins a paper sent to the 1965 Geneva Consultation on 'Patterns of Ministry in Europe Today' with the words, 'In the D.D.R. society considers the pastor—if it takes any notice of him at all—as a functionary of a small and dying organization.'[29] It cannot be long now before the British public take a similar view, if indeed they have not already done so in the urban areas. To revert to the article referred to at the beginning of this chapter, the second complaint that leads to withdrawal is that 'the minister holds a position on the periphery of modern life.'[30] Can it be the nagging suspicion that this is in fact the case that lies behind the *malaise* of the ministry?

Certainly it is true that the Welfare State has taken over many of the useful functions once performed by the Church and its ministry. Without trying to pretend that poverty no longer exists, nor minimizing the first-class social work that is still being done by some branches of the Church, it is no longer necessary to distribute coal tickets at the end of the Women's Bright Hour in the Central Hall; Meals on Wheels save the parson's wife from having to run round with a bowl of hot soup; the Rotary Club will distribute the Christmas parcels to the old people; the Philanthropic Society will see that they make their wills legally and do not go short of blankets; the Darby and Joan Club, often possessing its own suite of premises, will entertain them with nineteenth-century monologues and trips to the Kilburn Empire. Cards and flashing lights are provided by this and that organization for old people and invalids to put in their windows in case of emergency. Every social organization has its busy team of sick visitors. What is there left for the Church and her ministers to do?

Some would answer the question immediately by reference to the 'spiritual needs' which only the man of God can meet. In the case of the older people this would seem to be the right answer. The minister can go to the home and, among the china dogs and the prints of majestic stags in the Scottish Highlands, he can say a prayer and the good people will both understand it and be able to relate it to a valid and authentic experience of their own. But does the same thing happen with the younger generation? Is the pastoral prayer as readily acceptable and, to use the overworked word, as meaningful, in those homes where the china dogs and the stags at bay are replaced by Klees and Scandinavian furniture? It would be foolish to assert that it is never acceptable nor meaningful to the young, for that would be to contradict experience, but that it is becoming less and less so is hard to deny. The reason presumably is that here we are facing man who has come, or is coming, 'of age'. He has no 'spiritual needs' in the old familiar sense and the language that is used by those who suppose that he has, or believe that he ought to have, is, as van Buren said, meaningless, or largely so. This man has now ceased to come to church, for he thinks, as Bonhoeffer puts it, that 'more goes on in the cinema, it is really more interesting.'[31] The liturgy for this man will not be the Eucharist but the Saturday afternoon at White Hart Lane or Goodison Park with its intense sense of participation and involvement in something that is really being *done*. These are the people whom, according to Bonhoeffer, God is teaching to live without him and whose Christianity, if they have any, is of the religionless kind. It is not surprising that the traditional pastoral methods have no effect on those who do not share their basic presuppositions, nor that those who work on the assumption that they do will, unless they live in a cloud-cuckoo land, be disappointed and frustrated.

Another, and possibly baser, consideration must be mentioned at this point. Society is rapidly withdrawing the perquisites which once it bestowed upon the ministry. The cloth does not have the position nor enjoy the prerogatives which once it did. People do not treat ministers in the same respectful way. The contrast between the attitude to the 'meenister' in those more northerly and less 'secularized' parts of Scotland and that which one finds in a London coffee bar is significant. Daniel Jenkins looks at what lies behind the latter. 'The minister does not always have a clearly-defined status in society nor is there always a clearly-defined social expectation in relation to him.' The bank manager is there to provide real and relevant service, the dentist has a well-defined function to perform, the fireman is for putting out fires and the milkman for bringing round milk, but what is the minister *for*? To conduct weddings and funerals and preach to the dwindling few, but beyond that what? And if you don't know what he is for, how can you give him a status and accord him your respect? Jenkins goes on to argue[32] that this is a good thing, for he thinks that when a pattern of ministerial behaviour has become conventionalized it represents a measure of secularization. (Secularization for Jenkins is not the commendable thing it is to so many *avant-garde* writers. It is for him the regrettable sign that the Church is becoming conformed to this world which passes away.) One requires grace to accept the possibility that the loss of perquisites may be a good thing. If the grace is absent the fact that the world has withdrawn its prerogatives may help to harden the heart.

In Methodism preaching does not occupy the place which once it did, and this has not helped men who were trained to be preachers. Though in the modern theological college the other functions of the ministry are taken more into account, the older men submitted to the discipline of a study designed to make them preach well. Tears shed over Hebrew and Greek were reckoned to be worth it because the ability to expound the Bible in the sermon would be so much greater. Theology was taught to be assimilated and reproduced in more popular form in the sermon. Most Sundays students went out (and still do) to preach, and the sermon class and the 'trial' sermon in the college chapel were (and still are) regular and important features of college life. The aim was to produce Methodist preachers, and the crack preacher of the college enjoyed a status more exalted than the man at the top of the examination list. But preaching is not what it was. Although no one concerned to preserve the basic features of New Testament Christianity would wish to exclude from the essential marks of the Church the faithful proclamation of the Word, it is undeniable that the importance given to it in this generation is less than at any time since the Methodist revival. People no longer flock to hear the 'princes of the pulpit' in the full spate of their oratory. The 'popular preacher' who could fill the circuit or local chapel for the anniversary rally is becoming a rare bird. Only very occasionally in these days can churches be filled (or emptied) by the quality of the preaching. One reason for this state of affairs is that the language which must be used in a sermon to give expression to the redemptive acts of God and the desired response of faith is becoming increasingly difficult to relate to authentic experience, particularly among the younger generation. Another reason is that methods of communication have changed and if the pulpit insists on doing what those two formative influences, the television studio and the classroom, have rejected—standing up and talking to people non-stop for twenty minutes—the consequences have to be faced. But the main reason, and the one which links the decline in preaching with other phenomena which we have noticed in this chapter, is that the theological confusion we illustrated by reference to the Doctrine of God and the debate on Christian origins and the effect of this on Christian morality have tended to rob preachers of their authority. To stand up and preach, one must, without fundamentalism or blind dogmatism, be able to speak with authority. But today men are not as sure as their fathers were. Bonhoeffer is the patron saint of many, particularly younger, preachers and his comment on this is that 'the time when men could be told of everything by means of words, whether theological or simply pious, is over.'[33] It is not therefore to be wondered at that in such a situation the man who has been trained pre-eminently to be a preacher should feel the loss of a sense of purpose.

The more we enquire into the Methodist ministerial life, the more evidence we find for calling this chapter 'The Predicament of the Ministry'. Of course not every man will testify to this. Some have found that on the whole the Methodist system works well, they believe that they are exercising a useful and (to them) satisfying ministry and they have few grumbles. But if their experience was universal, or even that of the majority, we should not have a Professor of Theology telling us off the record that the Methodist ministry should be designated a 'national disaster area'. Unpalatable though it is, we have to draw attention to the weaknesses and the discontents.

The brotherhood of the ministry is an appreciated fact in the experience of many, but there are still men in the Methodist ministry who are lonely. It is frequently asserted by the more radical among us that the circuit system has broken down, and there is some truth in this. We are not here concerned with the usual questions—whether or not circuit boundaries correspond with the boundaries of real commitment and involvement—but with the state of the ministry. When men stayed only three years they had no time to settle down in a particular society and this made a circuit team possible, but now everybody stays longer and there is also a constant demand for pastorates and concentration in preaching and pastoral work. This demand is by no means unwise, but we have to face its concomitant, the loosening of the circuit bond. 'Team' work becomes less and less possible, though experiments are made here and there to turn back the tide, and the fellowship between the circuit ministers is not as deep. So men look to other groups to find it, to their ex-college cronies, to the Fellowship of the Kingdom, to Fraternals, to those with whom they work in the Methodist Peace Fellowship or the Methodist Sacramental Fellowship or the Methodist Revival Fellowship or to the particular District or Connexional Committee on which they serve. But not everybody falls in the way of such groups and some men are left alone. It is possible to be very lonely in the crowded coffee room before Synod begins.

Sometimes from his loneliness such a minister can brood over the faults and failures of the Church. In all probability he has had some unhappy experiences with church people and has encountered his share of bigotry, backbiting, humbug, cant and sheer cussedness. He may well compare this with the affability and tolerance that he finds in the cricket pavilion or in the golf clubhouse. He has to remember, naturally, that there are 'good and bad everywhere' and that it is easier to be good humoured when taking pleasure than when sitting through tedious meetings or fulminating against the impossible opinions of one's opponents in the debate on Anglican-Methodist relations. What constitutes the body blow in this situation is that in virtue of the Gospel and the claims of the Church to be a supernatural society, the church people ought to be different. And they're not.

Christian disunity may bolster the jaundiced view. The folly and sin of working in competition with other churches disheartens all those whose ecumenical eyes have been opened. It is made worse by the failure of most church people to see that there is anything wrong in it, and by their not being in the least concerned to have it changed. If one emerges from the station and walks through the delightful seaside suburb in which this book is being written, within a mile or so one can pass, or see just around the corner, ten Christian churches, eight of them equipped with a minister or priest, serving a population of some ten thousand living around them. No doubt they are all on the friendliest of terms but the eight ministers all know that once the suggestion is made that they should abandon their separateness and seek, as an incarnational religion must insist, to make visible their invisible unity in Christ, then the entrenched positions will be exposed and the theological battle will begin and, in all probability, never end. It is true that the minister has the progress of the Ecumenical Movement to encourage him, but the intolerable pressure of his local situation may more than cancel this out.

Of the ten Christian churches just referred to, only one is a Methodist. But elsewhere the picture is different. Fortunately the scandal of redundancy, the ex-Wesleyan Methodist, ex-United Methodist and ex-Primitive Methodist chapels which would, and in fact often do, die before they will unite, is slowly yielding to pressure. But is the pressure, particularly at the local level, due to a consciousness of the sin of division or is this another vindication of the Marxist view that all change is determined by economics? As far as the ministry is concerned, the years of redundancy, with their multiciplity of meetings, their raising of money for useless projects like decorating gaunt, ugly and unnecessary buildings, their almost total lack of vision and charity, were, and are, heart breaking.

It might be worth digressing at this point to ask whether or not the spiritual authority under which we work and the spiritual discipline to which we submit are adequate to deal with the discontents we are in the process of considering. Who is there to tell us to stop complaining and pray? Our Protestantism does not allow us a father-in-God who administers the sacrament of penance and gives spiritual direction, and the brotherhood of the ministry not infrequently fails, as we have seen, to provide the deep and intimate fellowship which can mediate a similar catharsis. The Chairman of the District can usually be relied upon to provide authority and advice in a crisis, but he could hardly be expected to provide the day-to-day spiritual discipline under which a minister ought to live. So we are thrown back upon our own resources. Unfortunately they depend upon the temperament, character and experience of the individual and the result is that those who are both well intentioned and well informed have an adequate private spiritual discipline and the rest of us don't. There is no office, there are no prayers which a Methodist minister has to say each day because he is a Methodist minister. Retreats, as distinct from conferences, are just beginning in Methodism, but we are a long way from the stage when every minister must go as part of the ministerial discipline. No one supposes that spiritual authority and discipline make discontented people contented, but it is foolish to toss aside a weapon so well tried in the wars. When are we going to treat this seriously?

But to return to the discontents: some men complain of the irrelevance to the real needs of society of so much that takes place in churches. They begrudge the long hours spent in making the machinery work and are convinced that the time has now come for a drastic streamlining of the structures so that time and energy can be found for the attempt to relate the Gospel to society. Men are impatient too with what they regard as trivialities in the life of the fellowship—the transparencies at the Guild of the holiday on the Costa Brava, the church social where lines of people on chairs pass a match-box cover from nose to nose to see who can finish first. Believing that the Church is 'for the world', they are depressed by the extent and hold of such inward-looking trivialities. They have come to the conclusion that many people outside the Church cannot see any relevance, and certainly no religious relevance, in the things which church people do and, sadly, they have come to agree with them.

'One of the first duties of advancing years is to stand up against the tyranny of dull drudgery.' [34] Frustration in the ministry is not the prerogative of angry young men. Men in the middle years can, as Oman suggests, be worn down by having to spend hours composing wording for posters, writing bits and pieces for newsletters, interviewing representatives from firms selling electronic organs, writing to architects, filling up interminable schedules and a thousand other things that could be adequately done by laymen. The ministry of the Word and Sacraments and the pastoral care of the flock of Christ inevitably suffer. Hubert Box tells the same story as an Anglican—'We are faced with the lamentable spectacle of priests who are snowed under by all manner of secondary things . . . things which they were not ordained to do, things which ought to be done by the laity.' [35]

Other ministers have been frustrated by meeting opposition to what they consider to be progress. One can sympathize with them. The tendency among most forward-looking ministers these days is to want some kind of liturgical reform. The 'hymn sandwich', the Communion as an optional epilogue, the 'right hand of fellowship' as the climax of 'Reception into full membership', the lack of audible and visible congregational participation even to the unwillingness to say 'Amen', these he will want to change. But even though he tries to lead and not to drive and introduces proper consultation at every stage, there will be a not inconsiderable number who will be quite intractable. The churches, says Daniel Jenkins, 'are notably affected by the conservatism of outlook which is natural in old-established societies', and English churches are probably among the worst. This failure to venture in faith is a damning indictment of a people who claim to live by faith. Liturgical reform is a clear example, though there are others, like missionary interest and evangelical concern. Sooner or later the question will be asked, 'Is it useful to go on battering one's head against a brick wall?' In this situation some men become impatient with the restrictions upon their authority demanded in the name of democracy. Here one thinks not of the occasions when a headstrong minister is restrained by a more cautious Leaders' Meeting, but of the occasions when a progressive minister is thwarted by conservative and apathetic laymen. The minister wants the authority to do his job as he sees it should be done, but the authority is not his to have. Some men begin to wonder at this point whether an authoritarian and hierarchical system might not be preferable to the strain of keeping up the appearance of democracy.

Other men have fallen foul of the invitation system and the decisions of the invitations committee. The minister's future and the well-being of his wife and family are in the hands of this committee. Doubtless it tries its best to be both just and kind, frequently with success, but it has to be admitted that in many circuits it contains people whose conception of the purpose of the ministry is sadly lacking. Notice must be taken of them, especially if they represent the 'smaller societies'. If a decision is taken against a minister he may smart under a sense of injustice, particularly as he has had no opportunity whatever to state his case. And the matter is not made any easier if he happens to be one of those who, because of its alleged failure to meet the pastoral situation, view the itinerant system with serious misgivings.

Others have allowed the iron to enter into their souls because of the personal privation which they contend has to be suffered by the minister and his family. The money, they say, is inadequate. The wife has to work. The children suffer, not merely because money is scarce but because father is always out and has no time to play cricket on the lawn. A day off every week seems impossible to engineer. Saturday is the day when the family are around, but father is so often either marrying people or slogging it out at circuit rallies, local preachers' schools, missionary workers' conferences, Sunday school teachers' training courses and the rest of the Saturday pastimes of the faithful.

But surely the greatest frustration of them all is that when a minister, in some moment of retreat or reassessment, turns from the trials and disappointments of his ministry to ask the basic question, 'What then *is* a minister?', the Methodists, not unlike others, are unable to give him a clear and satisfying answer. One will tell him that he is simply a layman working full time; another that he is what he is because he has received a call from God, ratified by the Church, to exercise his particular gifts within a full-time ministry; another that what distinguishes him from a layman are the functions which he has to perform within the fellowship of the people of God; another that ordination means the creation of an *ordo* and that he is therefore different in *being* from a layman. These different views of the ministry will be considered later. At the moment we must simply notice that at the precise point where the confusions should be cleared and the frustrations relieved, exactly the opposite happens.

Listing the causes of confusion and frustration in the

ministry is a depressing activity both for the writer and the reader. It is obviously one sided for nothing has been said of the answers that may well exist to the questions that have been asked and there has been no attempt to set the satisfactions of the ministry over against its frustrations. But this is of no consequence for there will be time and space for it later. The reason for beginning with the predicament of the ministry is that unless this is done one may be accused of holding that roseate view of the ministry which characterizes some of the blown-out articles in the popular religious press and which so anger the realistic and the radical. The impression given in these articles of which men complain is that ministers, or rather the kind whose work merits inclusion in these euphoric pieces, are never lost for new ideas and when they put them into practice they are invariably successful. The minister is, as the satirists used to say, a grand chap doing a grand job. It is not a far step from this to the unabashed personality cult that is still presented to us. Not all descriptions of ministers and their work are written at this turgid level and one must sympathize with the religious journalist who has to write what apparently people like to read, but the man who has been affected both by the theological and ethical ferment of our time and by the frustrations of the ministerial life knows very well that such roseate descriptions are far from the total reality. If we are to be of the slightest use to him we must begin with the recognition that the predicament of the ministry is not imaginary, but real.

REFERENCES

1 'Conversations between the Church of England and the Methodist Church.' *An Interim Statement*, pp. 26-7. SPCK and Epworth Press, 1958.

2 'Report 110' (1964-5), Home Mission Department of the Methodist Church.
3 *The London Quarterly and Holborn Review.* Epworth Press, July 1964.
4 *Systematic Theology*, vol. II, p. 6. Paul Tillich. James Nisbet, 1957.
5 *Biblical Religion and the Search for Ultimate Reality*, p. 82. Paul Tillich. James Nisbet, 1955.
6 Ibid., p. 13.
7 Ibid., p. 13.
8 Ibid., p. 83.
9 *The Secular Meaning of the Gospel*, p. 84. Paul van Buren. SCM Press, 1963.
10 *The London Quarterly and Holborn Review*, pp. 182-3. Epworth Press, July 1954.
11 *Theology of the New Testament*, vol I, pp. 26-7. Rudolf Bultmann. SCM Press, 1952.
12 Ibid., p. 26.
13 *The Interpretation of the New Testament*, 1861-1961, p. 243. Stephen Neill. Oxford University Press, 1964.
14 *Secular Christianity*, p. 104. Ronald Gregor Smith. Collins, 1966.
15 Ibid., pp. 102-3.
16 Ibid., p. 103.
17 *The Scrolls from the Dead Sea*, p. 98. Edmund Wilson. W. H. Allen, 1955.
18 Ibid., p. 129.
19 *The Dead Sea Scrolls*, chapter 10. J. M. Allegro. Penguin Books, 1956.
20 Ibid., chapter 11.
21 Ibid., p. 161.
22 *The Dead Sea Scrolls*, pp. 327-8. Millar Burrows. Secker and Warburg, 1956.
23 Ibid., p. 343.
24 *Honest to God*, p. 107. John A. T. Robinson. SCM Press, 1963.
25 *Sex and Morality*, A Report to the British Council of Churches. SCM Press, 1966.
26 *Soundings*, p. 80. Ed., A. R. Vidler, 1962.
27 *Moderate Drinkers and Total Abstainers*. Kenneth Greet. Epworth Press, 1963.
28 *The Basis of Pacifist Conviction*, p. 6. R. J. Billington. Fellowship of Reconciliation.

29 *Patterns of Ministry in Europe Today.* Paper to 1965 Geneval Consultation. Pastor Althausen. World Council of Churches Division of Studies, 1965.
30 *New Directions*, p. 12. Winter 1965.
31 *No Rusty Swords*, p. 154. Dietrich Bonhoeffer. Collins, 1965.
32 *The Protestant Ministry*, p. 98. Daniel Jenkins. Faber and Faber, 1958.
33 *Letters and Papers from Prison*, Second Edition, p. 122. Dietrich Bonhoeffer. SCM Press, 1956.
34 *Concerning the Ministry*, p. 237. J. Oman. SCM Press, 1936.
35 *Priesthood*, p. v. Hubert Box.

Chapter II

THE NATURE OF THE MINISTRY

To attempt to find answers to the confusions and frustrations one by one would probably be an inconclusive and certainly a tedious affair. We must go straight to the question that underlies all the others, and which, if it can be answered satisfactorily, will make all the others soluble, or if not soluble, at least bearable. What then *is* a minister? If we are sure we have the right answer to that question, then the assertion that the bones of Jesus are still in Palestine is the beginning of a fascinating theological exercise and not another nail in the ministerial coffin, and Christian disunity evokes not a lethargic depression but a zeal for the ecumenical movement. One can even live at peace with the bigots and the humbugs. But the basic question must have an answer.

No Methodist, one imagines, would wish to quarrel with the contention that the Methodist ministry is a charismatic ministry; that Methodist ministers are the recipients of some of the gifts of the Holy Spirit for ministry that are listed in the New Testament. I Corinthians 12 speaks, among others, of the gifts of wisdom, knowledge, faith, healing and prophecy. After the metaphor (if St Paul can fairly be said to use metaphors) of the body and its members there are listed the members of the charismatic ministry—apostles, prophets, teachers, healers, helpers, administrators and others. Ephesians 4:11 says the same thing: 'And his (the Ascended Christ's) gifts were that some should be apostles, some prophets, some evangelists, some pastors and teachers, for the equipment of the saints, for the work of ministry, for building up the body of Christ' (R.S.V.). Whether the gifts are thought of as natural endowments offered to God as part of the minister's 'reasonable, holy and living sacrifice' or as direct bestowals of the Spirit in answer to corporate or private prayer is for the moment beside the point. The point is that Methodists (like others) look for such gifts in their ministers. The ministerial session of the Synod, trying to make up its mind about sending a young man forward, has to ask itself the question: Has he wisdom, knowledge, faith, in embryonic if not in mature form? The Circuit invitation committee, considering a man for the circuit staff, will want to know how gifted he is as, to use St Paul's nouns, a prophet, an evangelist, a pastor, a teacher. The statement of C. H. Hwang that 'the set-apart ministry is essentially related to the special charismata within the charismatic body'[1] would not be criticized by most Methodists. No doubt on occasions Methodists have shown preference for the more showy and less 'spiritual' gifts, but such aberrations do not detract from the view—indeed they confirm it—that the minister must be a gifted man. He must be endowed, if possible liberally, by the Spirit.

This is sound enough as it stands. No one, in the light of the New Testament evidence, can deny the importance of the *charismata*. But if people go on to assume that such gifts are the constitutive element of the ordained ministry; that a man is a minister simply and solely because he is so gifted, then this must be contradicted. For quite plainly the *charismata* are generously distributed among the laity. Many class leaders have wisdom, knowledge, and faith not necessarily inferior to their minister's. Lay preachers have, in varying degrees, the gift of prophecy. The gift of healing seems quite unrelated to the clerical collar. But the main point to be grasped is that a clear distinction must be made between gifts for ministry bestowed by the Spirit and the commission to the Ministry* which, among other things, it is the purpose of ordination to give. The former is shared with the laity but the latter (by definition) is not. As the authors of the World Council of Churches Study Booklet, *Christ, the Holy Spirit and the Ministry*, put it,[2] 'Every Christian may receive a charisma, but some Christians receive in addition from the same Spirit a "special commission" to a particular task.' This was so in the New Testament and it is so now. The commission is related to the *charismata*, which may either precede or follow it, but it is not the same thing at all. As Basil Moss says, 'The nature of ordination itself must not be confused with the aptitudes proper to it.'[3] This is confirmed by the WCC Study paper just referred to. 'The state and authority of ministers are not based on charismata. . . . Nevertheless there is an intimate connection between the state and authority of a minister and the charismata he must "rekindle" and "not neglect" (I Timothy 1:6).'[4] So to answer the question, 'What is a minister?', by saying he is a man (or woman) who has received gifts from the Holy Spirit is, though in all probability factual, not adequate.

We must now take a long, hard look at a view of the ministry which is generally acceptable to most Methodists, and indeed to most Free Churchmen. We can call it the 'functional' view, because, though it takes various forms, the basis of it is that a minister is essentially a person who has been authorized to perform certain functions on behalf of the church. This is his *differentia*. He is not a layman because he performs functions which are generally (though most who hold this view would say not invariably) reserved to ministers. The Methodist minister is *par excellence* a functionary.

This view has its roots in the theological conviction that

* The capital letter is used here simply to distinguish the two uses of the word ministry in the one sentence.

the essential ministry is the ministry of the whole Church, or, to be more precise, the whole Church participating in the ministry of Christ. There has been a rediscovery of this in recent years and two modern statements can be quoted. First, the North American Section of the Report of the Theological Commission of the World Council of Churches on 'Christ and the Church': 'All in the Church are ministers in that they participate by grace through the gift of the Holy Spirit in the originative and determinative ministry of Christ; and the whole life of the Church is itself a ministry marked by many varieties of ministering.'[5] Second, the Statement of the Second Consultation on Theological Education in South East Asia (Hong Kong 1965): 'We have been reminded that there is but one ministry, the ministry of God Himself who in Christ has reconciled and is reconciling the world in all its dimensions to Himself, and has entrusted this ministry to His people *as a whole*'[6] (my italics). The Statement then goes on to assert that this one ministry is particularized in the *charismata* given to the members of the Church and then to complain that this broad and flexible diversity of ministries has been narrowed into a single, professional, ordained ministry. In the local church, it argues, the participation of the whole congregation in the total ministry of the Church has not been fulfilled.

We must at this point take up again the reference made in the previous chapter to the Liturgical Movement. With its emphasis upon the corporate nature of Christian worship and the participation in it of the whole *laos* of God it is in part responsible for this rediscovery and re-emphasis in our day of the view that the ministry is essentially the ministry of the whole Church. (This creates the odd situation in which those who by instinct abhor the Liturgical Movement as a seduction into the arms of the scarlet woman now find it their ally in resisting a sacerdotal ministry.) The doctrine of the priesthood of all believers is invoked in support of this view. The perverse interpretation of it, that there simply is no difference between ministers and laymen, is rejected and its true meaning, that every believer who has submitted, or been submitted, to what has been called 'the ordination of baptism' is a participant in the ministry of the Church, is advanced. 'Through our Baptism Christ incorporates us and ordains us for participation in his ministry.'[7] It is the whole people of God who are the 'royal priesthood' (I Peter 2:9). 'The whole Church is a priestly Body, since it has received its character from Christ the High Priest himself and exercises its ministry to all mankind in His Name and through His Spirit.'[8] Advocates of this view would emphasize that this is a rediscovery rather than a discovery, for the theological conviction that the essential ministry is the ministry of the whole Church is rooted in the New Testament. There the ministry of Christ in reconciling men to God is given to the whole company of believers and though there are 'varieties of gifts', 'varieties of service' and 'varieties of working' (I Corinthians 12:4), all given and inspired by the Holy Spirit, they are a participation in the total ministry of the whole people of God.

The functional view of the ministry is arrived at by a particular definition of this participation. The minister is said to participate in the total ministry of the Church by being authorized to perform certain functions in a representative capacity. This is the view of the ministry set out in the Deed of Union of the Methodist Church. Paragraph 30, which contains the 'doctrinal standards', asserts the priesthood of all believers, denies that a priesthood exists 'which belongs exclusively to a particular order or class of men', raises its hat to the charismatic ministry by saying that 'in the exercise of its corporate life and worship special qualifications for the discharge of special duties are required', and then proceeds to make the Methodist minister a functionary by adding 'and thus the principle of representative selection is recognized'. In other words the *esse* of the ministry is that its members should perform those special functions and duties which the Church has authorized them to perform on its behalf.

This is the conception of the ministry for which Daniel Jenkins contends in *The Protestant Ministry*.[9] The purpose of the minister, he says, is that he is 'set apart to be more or less "full-time" what other men are able to be only occasionally, a representative man.' This means no priesthood differing in kind from that of other men. The minister, continues Jenkins, 'has a special calling with its own specific and limited functions' and to this 'representative vocation' he must be faithful. The pastoral and devotional implications of this make clear what everyone acquainted with the Methodist ministry will know, that to be a functionary is not incompatible with being a true shepherd of the flock of Christ, though that is not to say that the functional view of the ministry is itself an adequate one.

What then are the functions which this representative man has to perform? What is he selected for? We will give Daniel Jenkins the first word. With the Acts of the Apostles never far from his mind he lists what he believes to be the functions of the ministry.

What is essential in any circumstances is that the Word should be faithfully preached and the sacraments administered according to Christ's ordinance, that the Church should be led to the place where it can discern the Spirit's guidance for its own life, that it should be kept of one heart and mind with the Great Church, that it should be built up in love and that, through its general apostolic ministry, many should be added to the number of those who are being saved.

This is as succinct a summary of the ministerial functions as we are likely to find and one with which few Methodists would disagree. The 'Word of God purely preached' and 'the Sacraments duly administered' are two of the marks of the true Church of the Reformation Confessions and though in the Methodist Church there is a certain sharing of these functions (the former as normal practice, the latter only in cases of ineluctable necessity) with the laity, the performance of them is always thought of as essential for the minister. To preach the Word and administer the Sacraments is what a minister is for. This clearly involves the wider function of leading and conducting the common worship of the people of God and, though 'Catholics' and 'Protestants' would think differently on the subject of the minister as a functionary, they would agree that there is a liturgical function which properly belongs to the ministry.

The work which in recent years has had most influence in representing the function of the ministry 'that the Church should be *led* (my italics) to the place where it can discern the Spirit's guidance for its own life' is Anthony T. Hanson's *The Pioneer Ministry**. The argument of the book is that the ministry, inheriting the functions of the Old Testament Remnant, 'shows in miniature what the Church should be.'[10] It pioneers the way. It has to live out 'the suffering, redeeming life of Christ in the world, in order that the Church as a whole may do likewise.'[11] There is no suggestion here,' adds Hanson, 'of the ministry doing anything which the Church as a whole cannot do; it is rather that the ministry is the pioneer for Christian living for the Church, as Christ was the pioneer for all of us.' The pattern therefore is 'Christ—the ministry—the Church',[12] and its place in this pattern is what gives the ministry its apostolicity. 'The ministry is only apostolic in as far as it carries out its task of leading the Church into the Church's apostolic task.'[13] While not all of Canon Hanson's thesis

* Reference to this work must not be taken to mean that Canon Hanson's view of the ministry can be contained within the meaning of the adjective 'functional'.

commands assent from scholars—Dr John Line, for example, would question the assertion that the first ministry *was* the Church, for he says that there were other things prior to the Church and that 'the Ministry arguably was one among them'[14]—there are not many who would wish to refute his main contention that one of the functions of the ministry is to pioneer the way to the place where the Church can 'discern the Spirit's guidance for its own life'.

Daniel Jenkins' summary goes on to say that one of the functions of the ministry is to act as the link between the local church and what is variously described as 'the Great Church', 'the universal Church', 'the One, Holy, Catholic, Apostolic Church'. This was reaffirmed in a European Consultation on the ministry held under the auspices of the World Council of Churches in John Knox House, Geneva, in September 1965, attended by the representatives of fourteen churches in eight countries. Their statement on 'The Special Function and Responsibility of the Ordained Ministry'[15] contains these sentences: 'The ordained Ministry has, however, in almost all traditions, the special function of representing the universal Church in a distinctive and articulate way, to the local Christian congregation and to the world alike. We recognize with penitence that the performance of this function is obscured by the present divided state of the churches.' This representative function has a long history, for in the early centuries of the Church's life the bishop represented his diocese in Ecumenical Councils and brought to his diocese the fullness and catholicity of the Church. He was responsible to both at once and it is this function that has been extended to the ordained presbyterate. The working minister is only periodically given the opportunity of representing his flock to a wider audience, but he is daily translating into the local language the customs, the theology, the liturgy and the devotion of the whole Church of Christ.

Pastoral work is the means by which the ministry carries out the function 'that it (the Church) should be built up into love'. In love and compassion the minister has to shepherd the flock of Christ. The Methodist Church has traditionally extended this function to the laity and the faithful Methodist class leaders, though now thin on the ground, demonstrated by the quality of their pastoral work the wisdom of this sharing. The official Methodist view is to assert on the one hand that the minister has 'no exclusive title to . . . the care of souls' and on the other to see he has his rightful place in the hierarchy of functionaries by saying that 'Christ's ministers in the Church are . . . Shepherds of His flock. Some are called and ordained to this sole occupation and have a principal and directing part in these great duties.'[16] This is consistent with a functional view of the ministry.

The Minister must perform his pastoral function in the form of a servant. All Christians are called, like their Lord, to be servants and to share in his self-giving ministry (Philippians 2:7) and this finds expression for the minister in his pastoral office. As Dr Line points out, the ministry has no caste status or right of privilege for 'The Ministry is set apart for service; in one of its essential aspects it is the Servant of the Church, chosen and appointed by it.'[17] Through the whole range of pastoral practice—the building up of relationships of understanding and trust, the house prayers and the sick Communions, the marriage counselling, the setting forth of the Gospel in word and compassionate deed at times of crisis, the fatherly concern about, and care for, the people of God—in all this the minister takes the form of a servant so that he can carry out in the spirit of his Lord the function which the Church has assigned to him.

The last function of the ministry listed by Daniel Jenkins is that it should lead the Church in mission. 'Through its (the Church's) general apostolic ministry, many should be added to the number of those who are being saved.' This is an optimistic definition of 'mission' in a secular society and Bonhoeffer's view of the Church as simply existing to 'take her part in the social life of the world, not lording it over men, but helping and serving them'[18] is probably more realistic. But whether 'mission' is conceived in terms of the older evangelism or of the Church as the suffering servant of the secular world, it is the ministry that must lead, direct, and inspire 'mission'. This is part, and possibly the most important part, of the function of Anthony Hanson's pioneering ministry. Quoting with approval the dictum of Dr M. A. C. Warren, 'The Church is mission', he argues: 'The ministry is the apostolic mission of the Church: its task is essentially pioneer, it is the spearhead of the Church.'[19] This function will be carried out in very different ways—one has only to contrast East Germany with West Germany to realize how varied the expressions of 'mission' can be—but that this is a proper ministerial function few will question. Both the Gospels and the Acts leave us no room for doubt.

We have described the functions of the ministry at more length than is strictly necessary in order that the functional view may be fully and fairly stated.* In this view, the answer to the question 'What *is* a minister?' is that he is, according to the principle of representative selection, set aside to perform the functions of preaching the Word, administering the Sacraments, directing the worship, pioneering the way forward, linking the local church with the One, Holy, Catholic Church, caring for the flock of Christ and leading the Church in its apostolic mission. And in the absence of other, non-functional categories by which to define the ministry, particularly (with one exception to

* It should be noted that this view is not always a clearly defined entity.

which reference will be made later) in the Methodist Deed of Union,* when you have said that you have said everything.

The first criticism that can be levelled against this functionalist view is the difficulty of *defining* the ministry in terms of function when we find one minister performing different functions from another, and yet both are ministers. Some ministers may perform all those on Daniel Jenkins's list; others only a proportion; others may perform functions, and New Testament ones at that, which find no place in the list before us. (Nothing is said there about healing or teaching or administration, all functions mentioned in I Corinthians 12.) The administrative official may do no pastoral work and the inward-looking, parochially-minded minister may never fulfil his function of leading the local church in its apostolic mission. How in this situation can the ministry be defined in terms of function? The question can be answered in two ways. Some will say that, though a complete list of ministerial functions can be extracted from the New Testament, in an imperfect world and an imperfect Church, with imperfect people, very few ministers can possibly fulfil them all. Ideally, all ministers ought to, but practically it is impossible. For the good of the Church most must concentrate on a limited number of functions. But this in no way invalidates their ministry. Others, less convincingly, select a number of 'basic' functions—preaching, administration of the Sacraments and pastoral care are the favourites—and assert that these are essential.

The first answer is satisfactory as far as it goes and can only be set aside as inadequate if later on we are able to

* It has been argued that something more than 'functionalism' (what one theologian has called representativeness) can be read into the 'principle of representative selection' of the Deed of Union and into the statement that 'a Minister . . . is the representative of the whole people of God' in the Statement on Ordination in the Methodist Church.[20] But it is difficult to substantiate this from the documents.

make out a theological case against the functional view as such. The second answer can more easily be dismissed. The selection of 'basic' functions from all those found in Scripture is quite arbitrary. Who is to say that celebration of the Sacraments should be in and leadership in mission out? In practice nobody accepts this view. Does anybody seriously believe that an ordained church administrator spending long hours behind an office desk who never makes a pastoral call from one year's end to another is no longer a minister? And what of the ordained teacher, head of the R.K. department in a large comprehensive school? It can reasonably be argued that his teaching is an extension of the ministry of the Word, but long months may go by before he celebrates the Communion and he may never baptize a baby again. Is he therefore no longer a minister? Those who deny it—and they are few—do so, not because they have a considered theological case, but because for one reason or another they disapprove of men leaving the 'regular' ministry of the Church.

The second difficulty of defining the ministry functionally is that there are laity in the Church as well as ministers and that many 'ministerial' functions are performed by them. In the Methodist Church laymen and laywomen preach the Word, care for the flock of Christ and in some places and situations lead the local church in its apostolic mission. This is recognized officially in the Deed of Union: 'These ministries (preaching the Gospel and the care of souls) are shared with them (the ordained ministry) by others to whom also the Spirit divides his gifts severally as he wills.' That the laity participate in the total ministry of the Church by performing functions (and receiving gifts) which are frequently attributed to the ordained ministry may well be a cause for rejoicing in this age of 'the layman's church', but it hardly facilitates the definition of the ministry on the basis of function. To reply that a minister can fulfil all the functions, in theory if not in practice, and a layman only some, is not convincing, for we are left to sort out which are ministerial functions and which lay, a considerable feat in a Church which in certain circumstances—one thinks of the old 'lay pastors' with dispensations to administer the Sacraments—allows laymen to perform them all. The Deed of Union provides a lame answer at this point for, as we have noticed, after saying that Christ's ministers in the Church are Stewards in the household of God and Shepherds of His flock, it adds that ministers are called and ordained 'to this *sole* occupation and have a *principal* and *directing* (my italics) part in these great duties', as if the difference between a minister and a layman were simply the amount of time put in on the job. This has been recognized by others. The Report of the Working Party of the British Council of Churches, 'The Shape of the Ministry',[21] speaks of 'the identification of *minister* with *full time minister*, supremely seen in the practice of the Methodist Church'. Does the *esse* of the ministry lie in the time sheet?

We ought to turn aside for a moment at this point to take brief notice of the views of John Calvin, because he is one of the traditional upholders of the position we are examining and it can fairly be said that he represents it at its best. Calvin thought of the ministry in terms of function. He spoke of God 'employing men to perform the function of his ambassadors in the world'[22], and he distinguished four main functions—the function of the pastor in preaching and administering the Sacraments, of the doctor in testing and teaching, of the elder in shepherding and exercising discipline, of the deacon in showing compassion. And as Wilhelm Niesel says, 'He recognized from Holy Scripture that these various functions must be permanently fulfilled if the church is to expand and be preserved.'[23] There is also a charismatic element in Calvin's view, for, to quote Niesel again, 'The pre-requisite for the bestowal of an office is that the person concerned shall have the necessary capabilities.'[24]

We can claim that Calvin took this view of the ministry because his position was determined by his reaction from Rome and by the sociological situation in which he was placed. But it is more to the point, if we can say so without anticipating too much the trend of our own argument, that Calvin's view is not that the ministry is *only* charismatic and functional. In the middle of all his words on the functions of the ministry he writes of God using 'the ministry of men, by making them, as it were, his substitutes'[25] and of having ministers 'to represent his (God's) own person.'[26] He refers not only to modes of service and functions but also to 'the apostolical and pastoral office'. The preachers of the Word not only fulfil the function of preaching, they 'represent the Person of the Son of God.'[27] We can therefore defend ourselves if Calvin is quoted against us by saying that, not only have the circumstances that gave rise to his theology changed beyond recognition, but even the briefest glance at his work shows that there is more to his doctrine of the ministry than what we have here described as 'functional'.

Many people who are inclined towards a functionalist view of the ministry will not regard the substance of the preceding paragraphs as important for they see little reason to define the ministry at all. As long as a man is doing the job and fulfilling the functions what does it matter how you define him? The part-time lay preacher, the self-appointed pastors of evangelical sects, are all to be regarded as ministers. It is thought to be a sign of the legalistic mind if questions are asked about the validity of such ministerial orders. Isn't it enough that they are doing a good job for the Lord? Those who, because of their 'catholic' views, wish to go beyond functions successfully performed to consider abstruse questions about the *esse* of a minister are put in the same category as the Pharisee who criticized the ministry of Jesus (John 9:29) and the doctors who scoff at successful spiritual healers.

We can begin to move away from this rather naïve position by noticing, on a broader front, that what a person *does* is not the only thing that matters. The clearest example is that of man himself. To think of man only in terms of his functions in society, his usefulness to the community, is to downgrade him. Christians believe—whatever some psychologists say—that man has a status *as man*, quite apart from what he does or does not do, and to this his functions are secondary. Bishop Lesslie Newbigin takes up this point in his *Honest Religion for Secular Man* and gives the illustration of Hitler sending men to the famous Bethel Hospital to inform Pastor Bodelschwingh, its director, that the state could no longer afford to maintain hundreds of epileptics who were useless to society and only constituted a drain on scarce resources, and that orders had been issued to have them destroyed. Bodelschwingh would have none of it, for even if these people could perform no useful function they must be respected simply as men and women. As Bishop Newbigin puts it, 'He had no other weapon for that battle than the simple affirmation that these were men and women made in the image of God and that to destroy them was to commit a sin against God which would surely be punished.'[28] To think of man purely in functional terms does not necessarily lead to this kind of brutality, but it is always to do man less than justice.

Could not this also be true of the ministry? If it is, the reason, to use the old terms for a moment, is that *being* is prior to, and more important than, *doing*. The acts of God are determined in their nature and quality by the kind of Being God is, and though God may be known through his acts, he is himself distinct from them. The Work of Christ is closely related to the Person of Christ, but they are not the same. Christ may be known in and through his work, but he has a reality apart from it. The functional view of the ministry denies or ignores this distinction as far as the ministry is concerned. It equates *being* and *doing*. The only ontology it grants to the minister is his ontology as a man. His ministry is simply a matter of a man doing things. The question is whether or not we can deny any *being* to the ministry so easily.

Must the answer to the question 'What *is* a minister?' then be that in some sense a minister is different in *being* from a layman? In considering this we have to take pains to see that we do not become entangled in the kind of argumentation about the nature and extent of *being* that characterized the philosophical side of medieval scholastic theology. There *being* was conceived of in a substantial fashion—a kind of philosophical glue that fastened all the bits and pieces of an entity together—and we must not try to stick the ministry together with ancient philosophical glue. Fortunately there is little temptation today to argue the case in favour of a minister being *different* by recourse to the medieval terms. But sometimes where an essential difference is denied—as Nikos Nissiotis denies it for the Orthodox[29] and as many Methodists would deny it—it is possible that the old terms are still affecting judgements. Perhaps therefore it would be as well to drop the word *being* with its medieval overtones and to use more conceptual language. This view can then be stated in terms of a difference of conception. Can we not say that a minister is different from a layman because he is conceived to be different? And as this question presents an obvious temptation to be quoted out of context with the accusation that things don't happen to be different just because we like to think they are, can we not go on to say that a minister is conceived to be different because of certain events that have happened in which he has been deeply involved and which in fact have made him different? Let us look at these events.

The first is that the minister is called into the ministry. Although the Methodist Deed of Union goes out of its way to deny any difference (in kind) of priesthood between ministers and laity, and to assert the functional view, the one step it does take in an ontological direction (and this is the exception referred to above) is in its insistence upon the minister's call. 'It is the universal conviction of the Methodist people that the office of the Christian Ministry depends upon the call of God who bestows the gifts of the Spirit the grace and the fruit which indicate those whom He has chosen.' But a call is divisive. It separates A from B. One is taken and the other left. In this sense A is *different* from B.

It is impossible to read the Bible in this context without becoming aware of how central is the operation of vocation. Israel was above all things a Chosen People. Abraham and his seed, Noah and his little community in the ark, Moses and his 'nation', they were elected by God and the consciousness of election, though temporarily blurred by unfaithfulness, was, thanks to the faithful Remnant, never lost. Within the chosen community a further process of calling can be discerned. The tribe of Levi and the house of Aaron are called to perform priestly functions on behalf of the whole body of the people and leaders like Abraham and Moses and David and, of course, the prophets, are the objects of election. I Samuel 3 (the call of Samuel) and Isaiah 6 (the call of Isaiah), as well as being among the best-known passages of the Old Testament are (and perhaps this is the reason) epitomes of how God deals with his people, individually as well as collectively. He calls them. In the New Testament the Church has taken the place of Israel as the Chosen People of God. The entire community is chosen in Christ from the foundation of the world.

Christians are 'called to belong to Jesus Christ' (Romans 1:6). They are 'called to be saints' (I Corinthians 1:2). They are 'to lead a life worthy of the calling to which (they) have been called' (Ephesians 4:1). Within the community there were those apostles who had been called by Christ in Galilee. Then there were those commissioned to some of the various ministries* which later characterized the life of the early Church; they too were the objects of God's gracious election. Paul was called on the road to Damascus, Timothy was called 'with a holy calling' (II Timothy 1:9). At the making up of the number of the Apostles in Acts 1, the petition is 'Lord, who knowest the hearts of all men, show which one of these two Thou hast chosen to take the place in this ministry and apostleship' (vv. 24, 25). The reception of a call as one of the distinguishing marks of the ministry rests on a solid biblical foundation.

It is important to stress at this point that the difference existing in virtue of the fact that one man has been called and another has not, is not a difference of status. This was the lesson that Israel had to learn. Her election did not mean exaltation over others. 'Ministers of the Church are wrongly set *over above* the people.'[31] Dr John Line emphasizes this and gives the New Testament evidence for it. 'The Ministry', he says, 'does not acquire "rank" in having its own being and calling. Be not called Rabbi, commands Jesus, ye are all brethren (Matthew 23:1-12).' The ministry is called to service, not to exaltation. Dr Line continues, 'The Ministry we have said is distinct, or in Paul's word "separated". But the separation is positive in the Church's life. . . . Separation is the divine ordainment

---

* 'In the New Testament, and especially in Acts and in the Pastoral Epistles, the Apostles, but not only the Apostles, are spoken of as receiving a special calling from God, which is confirmed by the Church. This commission is never for such services as healing or speaking with tongues, rather is it for the service of establishing the Church and of leading it.'[30]

and quality of the Ministry for service to all who are called in the Gospel, not for being raised officiously above them (Mark 10: 43, 44).'[32] It was this truth that was sometimes forgotten in Israel but must not be omitted when trying to see that vocation has a proper place in a doctrine of the ministry.

What is most significant, however, about a call is that it is an event planned and carried through by God. Intimations of the call may come through various human channels—through the knowledge that in the Church today there are not enough men offering themselves for the ministry, through the recognition, in humility, of the presence in oneself of the gifts and graces normally required for the ministry (the 'July Committee' exists to correct wrong impressions!), through encouragement given, and even pressure applied, by those who can make an objective assessment of one's character and abilities—but intimations do not constitute a call. The call comes direct from God. To say this is not to look for a vision in the night nor to hear heavenly voices in the bells, but it is to know and experience in an inward, 'religious' sense that God himself is 'putting on the pressure'. This is thoroughly biblical, for the prophet knows his call is from God and the apostle is the one who has been sent by Christ. The important thing to recognize is that where confusion exists and a man is not sure whether he is being called or not, the root of the confusion is in our human inability to recognize or test the call and not God's reluctance to make up his mind. God calls whom he wills. Our contention is that, because he has called one man and not another, we can and ought to conceive a difference existing between them. The called man is different just because he has been called.

The second event in which the minister has been deeply involved, and which makes his difference from the layman not only a matter of *charismata* and function, is ordination.

Ordination is more than an event, if by an event is meant something that once happened in a particular place at a particular time. Like baptism, it is a fact of history and a present experience. Like the Resurrection, it happened, but its present effects are quite as significant as its historicity. So our discussion on what difference is involved is set in the context not merely of a once-for-all mechanical act which makes a man different but of a continuing and unfolding experience of what Christ, through the Holy Spirit, means ordination to be.

The theology of ordination is so wide a subject, and of such importance in the present ecumenical debate, that to attempt to summarize even the major issues involved would be both a lengthy process, and one exposed to misunderstanding. It is preferable for our purpose to begin with the Methodist Ordination Service and to ascertain as clearly as one can the meaning of what is there said and done. What are the elements in this particular service which, as we claim, make a man different from that day forward?

The first is the prayer of the Church for those to be ordained. At one point in the service, there is a bidding of a general kind which, after making reference to Christ's prayer before choosing and sending forth the Twelve and the prayers of the disciples at Antioch before they laid hands on Paul and Barnabas, urges the congregation to 'fall to prayer before we admit and send forth these persons presented unto us to the work whereunto we trust the Holy Spirit hath called them.' There is a rubric following instructing the people to 'make their humble supplication to God for all these things', but the precise intention of these prayers is not specified. Elsewhere in the service prayer offered for the ordinands has more exact intentions. Prayers for faith, virtue, grace and gratitude are said. But central to the rite is prayer for the Holy Spirit. 'Fill them by the presence of Thy holy and life-giving Spirit, with all faith and love, all power and sanctification.' It is repeated in hymn form:—

> *O Source of uncreated heat,*
> *The Father's promised Paraclete,*
> *Thrice holy Fount, thrice holy Fire,*
> *Our hearts with heavenly love inspire;*
> *Come, and Thy sacred unction bring*
> *To sanctify us while we sing.*

As the statement *Ordination in the Methodist Church*[33] says, 'The Ministry is God's gift to his Church and the persistent prayers for the power of the Holy Spirit is a distinguishing mark of the whole service.'

If we now proceed to ask for what particular purpose the gift of the Holy Spirit is required, the answer is for the setting aside and appointment to the office and work of a minister (which is a participation in the ministry of the Spirit himself) and for the charismata necessary for the fulfilment of that office and work. As Dr Line puts it, 'The gift of the Spirit, that is, is not the Minister, his function already apportioned to him, receiving empowerment for it, but it is his being given the function with empowerment inherent to the gift.'[34] This means that neither the functional view nor the charismatic view of the ministry is adequate on its own and it leads us on to suggest that a man for whom these prayers have been answered and who has therefore both been appointed and equipped by the Holy Spirit to share in his own ministry must now be conceived as being different from those to whom this has not happened.

The desire, in the compilation of the Methodist Ordination Service, to avoid the slightest suggestion of sacerdotalism has had an unfortunate effect in relation to the gift of the Holy Spirit. At the moment of the laying-on of hands the Anglican ordinal says without equivocation,

'Receive the Holy Ghost for the office and work of a Priest in the Church of God', but the Methodist order has 'Mayest thou receive the Holy Spirit for the office and work of a Christian Minister and Pastor', so giving the impression that the petition is still being sent up instead of acknowledging the fact that the answer is being received. This is regrettable, for a company of Methodists, ordaining a man in faith and with prayer, should have as much assurance that their faith and prayer are rewarded as any other Christian body, and it would not be the intention of the service to deny this. In which case, if the Holy Spirit is then and there given and received it is surely perverse to argue that the ordinands are to be conceived as no different from what they were before.

This brings us to the rite of the laying-on of hands. It is biblical, but its meaning varies from place to place in Scripture. In the Old Testament it is sometimes used for the blessing of sons and grandsons, sometimes for the transmission of personal virtue and vitality, sometimes for the consecration of Levites, sometimes for the conferring of 'the dignity and personal authority that must go with high office.'[35] It is the consecration of the Levites which, in the Old Testament, throws most light upon the rite as it is used in ordination. Just as the worshipper in the temple laid hands on an animal to mark it out as the one to be sacrificed, so the Levites were separated for the service of God and, in virtue of that separation, they were different. In the New Testament the laying-on of hands continued. Christ laid hands on people in blessing and they were made whole. The Church in the Acts of the Apostles used the rite as one of appointment and commission and if one thinks of this not in terms of abstract *being* but empirically, it is obvious that a very considerable change took place in the lives of those concerned. It is also used to signify the bestowal and reception of the gift of the

Spirit. A text like I Timothy 4:14, 'Do not neglect the gift you have, which was given you by prophetic utterance when the elders laid their hands upon you' cannot make much sense to those who contend that at ordination nothing *happens*.

This biblical rite is at the centre of the Methodist Ordination Service. Apart from the gift of the Holy Spirit which has already been mentioned, a number of ideas are closely linked to it. One is that of commission. The office and work of a Christian Minister and Pastor is 'now committed unto thee by the imposition of our hands'. The Holy Spirit said to the congregation at Antioch, 'Set apart for me Barnabas and Saul for the work to which I have called them' (Acts 13:2), and this they did, for after fasting and praying 'they laid their hands on them and sent them off.' This is what happens to every Methodist who is ordained to the ministry and at the risk of being tiresome we must say again that in our conception of what a minister is we cannot equate the commissioned with the uncommissioned.

Next, at the moment of the laying-on of hands the command is given to the minister to be 'a faithful Dispenser of the Word of God'. The Methodist service is at this point following the Anglican Ordinal and though the sentence giving power of Absolution is omitted from this paragraph, the word 'dispenser' comes from that source. It is a word from Cranmer and his school who decided on spoken words during the laying-on of hands instead of the silence (*nihil dicens*) of the Roman rite. 'Dispenser', though not a biblical word, has at this point in the non-episcopal Methodist service to carry whatever notions of apostolicity we may read into Methodist ordination.

The ministry of the apostles was twofold. They were— and this is the point emphasized by Anthony Hanson—the nucleus of the Church, the pioneer community nourished by and committed to the Word and the Sacraments. They were also 'sent', commissioned by Christ himself to 'go and make disciples of all the nations' (Matthew 28:19), which meant inevitably giving pride of place to the preaching of the Word. This is the twofold apostolic ministry, continued in every age. The precise method of ensuring its continuity is not here under discussion, but as the Report of the Third World Conference on Faith and Order (Lund 1952) said, 'Most (and this certainly includes Methodists*) would . . . regard the preaching of the Gospel and the ministration of the Sacraments as essential means of continuity.'[36] To 'be a faithful Dispenser of the Word of God and of his holy Sacraments' means to continue in the apostolic ministry of building up the life of the Church (the strengthening function of Acts 18:23) and engaging in mission to the world. Methodist ministers are at their ordination 'sent' to their dispensing and this 'being sent' is, as Dr Line points out,[37] 'the essence of Apostleship and defines Apostolic Ministry'.

This is not the place to assess the varying views of scholars on the meaning of the Hebrew *shaliach,* but that there is a unity between the sender and the sent beyond the mere act of commissioning would seem to be clear from such texts as Matthew 10:19, 20—'What you are to say will be given to you in that hour; for it is not you who speak, but the Spirit of your Father speaking through you': Matthew 16:40—'He who receives you receives me, and he who receives me receives him who sent me': Luke 10:16—'He who rejects you rejects me': John 15:15—'All that I have heard from my Father I have made known to you': and John 15:20—'If they kept my word, they will keep yours also.' To be in an apostolic ministry, as Methodists would strongly claim that they are, is to be a partner in such a relationship. As Dr Line says,[38] 'To be joined with Christ,

* My brackets.

not just His representative but to be one with Him in Word and Power, is ever the existence and burden—and singular freedom—of the Apostolic Minister.' Is not this what is conferred on a Methodist when in the solemn rite he is commanded to be a faithful dispenser? Is he not at this point entering the apostolic ministry, and with it the *shaliach* relationship which that ministry has to Christ? The logic of the position would seem to be that if he is not then the Methodist ministry is in this respect deficient. But if he is, it can hardly be contended that the only difference between him and the unordained is that he spends all day doing what they only do in the evenings.

It is at this point, and on theological grounds, that the inadequacy of a purely functionalist view of the ministry is so evident. The *shaliach* relationship means that the ministry of the Catholic Church—which includes the Methodist ministry—is a continuation of Christ's own ministry. This is not confined to an act of commissioning in the sense that the disciples were commissioned to do precisely what Christ had been doing throughout his ministry on earth, and ministers ever since have been commissioned to do it too. When Christ spoke, as he is frequently recorded in the Fourth Gospel as having done, about the Father sending him, John usually expressed it in the aorist tense—5:23, 27; 6:44; 8:16, 18; 12:49; 14:24. But when in his Resurrection glory Christ related his own 'being sent' to the sending of the apostles (John 20:21), John puts the verb* into the perfect. The point is that the Father has sent Jesus and the sending still continues in the apostles. And to this there is no end. When Christ in the visible body returned to heaven at the Ascension then in the body of the apostolic ministry the eternal mission of the Incarnation was, and is, continued. Peter demonstrated

* A different one, but as C. K. Barrett says, 'the two verbs seem to be used synonymously in this gospel.'[39]

the truth of this when, as recorded in Acts 9, he went down to Lydda and was confronted with a bedridden man. 'Jesus Christ heals you,' he said. And Aeneas was healed. This was part of the continuing and never ending ministry of Christ exercised through his ministers. And without involving ourselves in an argument about the nature of succession we can say that the ministry of preaching, baptising, administering the bread and wine at the Table and caring for the flock of God is still Christ's ministry. As the Methodist statement on Ordination puts it (though it does not at this point relate it to the ordained ministry), 'Christ Himself, who took "the form of a servant" and "came not to be ministered unto, but to minister", continues His ministry in the world.'[40] It is this continuing ministry of Christ, through his called and ordained ministers that the functional view is unable adequately to express. Though, to quote again from the statement on Ordination, 'in the office of a Minister are brought together the manifold functions of the Church's ministry',[41] it is impossible, as one Methodist theologian has put it, 'to become a "vicar of Christ" by accumulating functions'. Functions do not add up to an office. But to be the representative of Christ, the instrument of his continuing ministry in the Church and in the world, is something which even the word 'office' cannot adequately express and it is at least arguable that this is what the Methodist statement on Ordination means when it says that 'a Minister is Christ's ambassador.'[42] The Methodist minister is a minister *of Christ*. Professor Kenneth Grayston, a Methodist, expressed this with clarity in an article he wrote for *New Christian**:

The ministry is there to ensure the real and total presence of Christ in the Church—audibly present in the preaching, visibly present in sacrament, effectively present in discipline and pastoral care. Here is Christ being heard, seen and effectively felt so that his whole

* 6 October, 1966.

ministry is performed. In particular, it must include his redeeming ministry which he accomplishes by suffering. All Christians *may* be asked to suffer redemptively in Christ's ministry; all ministers *are* separated to this work of redemptive suffering.

To speak of the ministry in these terms (ensuring the real, effective, redemptive presence of Christ) goes far beyond what any of us would claim for himself. Hence the constant Christian claim that in ordination God, acting in his Church, makes a man what otherwise he is not and could not be.

After the laying-on of hands comes the delivery of the Bible with the words 'Take thou authority to fulfil the office of a Minister in the Church of Christ.' The 1549 Prayer Book preserved the *traditio instrumentorum*, the rite of delivery to the ordinand of the chalice and paten for the Mass, but in 1552 and again in 1662 this was omitted in favour of the delivery of a Bible with the words 'Take thou authority to preach the Word of God, and to administer the holy Sacraments in the Congregation, where thou shalt be lawfully appointed thereunto.' This the Methodists have abbreviated.

Many ecumenical arguments have been waged as to who precisely in the Church has the authority to ordain Archbishop Temple's famous words on the consecration of bishops—and so by implication of the ordaining of priests— 'the authority by which I act is His, transmitted to me through his apostles and those to whom they committed it; I hold it neither from the Church nor apart from the Church, but from Christ in the Church' have caused considerable controversy. The Methodist position is perfectly clear. Authority resides in the Conference. 'The act of making a man a Minister is performed by the Methodist Conference, by its standing vote in the Reception into Full Connexion and through its appointed representatives in the Ordination Service; it is not performed by individuals, or a group of individuals, acting in their own capacity.'[43] But our concern here is not to argue who is the proper agent of authorization but simply to insist that a person who has been authorized by ordination within the One, Holy, Catholic Church of Christ must be conceived as different from one who has not. Of course it can be argued that anybody can pick up a Bible and claim that because he has it and can expound its truth he possesses the same authority as the minister. But this is both to ignore the words 'to fulfil the office of a Minister' and to wrench the act from the context of ordination. Once the Bible has been given, and these words said, the minister has—as no one else has—the full authority of the Church (which is the authority of the Word) for his ministry of Word and Sacraments.

It can be said in passing that it is both an encouragement to the minister and a salutary discipline to his people to remember that his authority to be a minister of the Word and Sacraments comes not from the validity of his own personal religious experience nor from his excellence of character, but from his ordination. This is not to discount personal experience and excellence of character nor to pretend that it is not important that a minister should possess them. But to understand that *authority* for the work of the ministry resides elsewhere—in the Word, given through the Church—might both comfort ministers in moments when they face their own sin and prevent the laity from confusing the validity and efficacy of a man's ministry with the kind of man he is.

The fact that such authority for the ministry of Word and Sacraments is given in ordination calls for a brief clarification of the Methodist position. If to ordain is to give authority to dispense the Word and Sacraments then the converse is true. To dispense the Word and Sacraments is the equivalent of being ordained. How does Methodism reconcile this with the fact that laymen are authorized to preach (frequently) and to administer the Lord's Supper (rarely)? The answer is that *episkope* in these matters resides in the Conference and it is this *episkope* that is here being exercised. The lay preacher is 'put on the plan' by the authority of the Quarterly Meeting which is exercising in a local situation the *episkope* of Conference. The layman who receives a dispensation to administer the Lord's Supper receives it, after a Synod vote, from the President acting on behalf of the Conference. This is all done properly and in order. Our criticism can only be that as yet it is not done sacramentally.

The last act associated with the laying-on of hands in the Methodist Ordination Service is the declaration by the President that the men are now ordained. 'In the name of our Lord Jesus Christ, the only Head of the Church, I hereby declare you to be ordained to the office of the Holy Ministry.' If words mean anything, these mean the creation of an *ordo* in the Church, a distinct order of ministry. This is supported by the fact that if Methodist ministers resign they do not lose their ordination. Their orders are simply 'in suspension'. If they return they are not 're-ordained' for 'ordination is never repeated in the Methodist Church.'[44] It is a positive, creative act, done once and for all. And those who belong to an *ordo* are, by definition, different from those who do not. Perhaps this is best understood if we look at it not from the Churchward side—the setting apart and commissioning of those who have been called—but from the Godward side. Here we are confronted not with a God who gives a charitable nod of his head in approval of what his Church is doing, but a God who is, because it is his nature to be, engaged in *creatio continua*, never-ceasing creative activity. We know and experience this in creation itself, in Baptism where he creates members of his Body, in the Eucharist and the preaching of the Word where he creates new men in Christ and at the Resurrection of the dead where he recreates us in a Resurrection body.

Are we to stifle the activity of this Creator on the day of ordination? It would seem more in keeping with what we know of his ways to believe that in this service he is *making* ministers.

In this attempt to demonstrate that the Ordination Service makes a difference to a man that is more than the bestowal of charismatic gifts or the conferring of the right to perform a function, the last section of the Service to be considered is the taking of the Ordination vows. The vows in the Methodist Service are both comprehensive and precise. They leave nothing unsaid, from the acknowledgement of the call of the Holy Spirit in the first to the promise to testify to the Gospel of the grace of God in the last. They range over the whole field of ministerial life—pastoral work, administration of the Sacraments, fidelity to Methodist doctrine, submission to discipline, diligence in the spiritual life, moral example and the care of the churches. They contain no ambiguities, but in each case come straight to the point and ask the question that calls for an unequivocal answer. Taken together they demand a commitment of the whole person for all time, and the overwhelming impression they give is that a man who has taken them is committed to such an extent that it is not merely playing with words to say that he is a different *kind* of man. Before the taking of these vows he could sit with a certain looseness upon their demands. In a sense he could please himself. But not afterwards. He is then a totally committed person and there may indeed be occasions during the arduous years of ministry when this commitment is the one thing that prevents him from resigning. When the frustrations and confusions mentioned in the previous chapter are at their worst he may well be kept in the ministry by the fact that he *vowed* to become and to remain a Methodist minister. Is he to be conceived as no different from someone to whom all this is a closed book?

The truth for which we are contending in this chapter is that the answer to the question 'What *is* a minister?' is not only that he possesses gifts of the Spirit and has been appointed by the people of God to carry out certain functions on their behalf, but that in virtue of his call and his ordination he is to be conceived of as essentially (ontologically) different from a layman. Again it must be stressed that this has nothing whatever to do with the establishment of clerical status or the desire for clerical privilege. The minister is a servant of the people of God, and a servant he must remain. And certainly it must be divorced from the assumption—though this is no plea for an antinomian liberty—that the minister is different *morally* from the layman. Perhaps the real difference can be expressed by saying that the minister is a sacramental person in a sense that a layman cannot be. The parallel with marriage is illuminating. The gay bachelor (laymen are reminded that this is an illustration, not an allegory!) may have the same gifts of friendship, of companionship, of making love as the married man. If he sits lightly to the moral code he may perform the same emotional and physical functions. But there is an essential difference between them. It is rooted not in what they are nor in what they do but in the fact that one is *married* and the other is not. And the one who is married is, simply in virtue of that fact, different. Roman Catholics, with their usual thoroughness, have taken this to its logical conclusion. So the 'whisky priest' of Graham Green's novels, degraded and debauched as he may be, possessing no gifts of the Spirit, and performing normally no ministerial functions, has only to take bread and wine into his hands or pronounce absolution over a penitent and, *because he is ordained,* the miracles of grace happen there and then. One does not have to subscribe to the Roman doctrine of the priesthood to accept that God, having called a man and, through his Church, ordained him, uses him, precisely in virtue of that call and ordination, to communicate the blessings of the Gospel.

The fact that the sacramental person is used in virtue of his call and ordination is a welcome move away from the personality cult and the subjective interpretation of the ministry which has had such a vogue in the Free Churches (and not only in them). Article XXVI of the Thirty-nine Articles, 'Of the Unworthiness of the Ministers which hinders not the effect of the Sacrament' expresses the truth that in Word and Sacrament the grace of God can come to his people even though the minister is an evil man. As the last paragraph of the Article demonstrates, this is not meant to be an encouragement to sin. On the contrary, recognition that one is used in this sacramental fashion should be a cause for gratitude to God and for renewed devotion. But it is an assertion that a man who is called and ordained to the ministry is used by God *because he is a minister*, and in some cases and instances, for that reason alone.

This is a view of the ministry which will not be readily acceptable to all Methodists. The charismatic view has a powerful influence among us and we are constantly being tempted to measure a man's ministry by the gifts he displays. The functional view is almost endemic to Methodists who are among the most busy Christians on earth. Ministerial functions are carried out for the most part, if one may say so, conscientiously and indeed with zeal and enthusiasm. But the notion that a minister exists not only for *doing* but for *being*; not only to *do* what a minister does in preaching, administering and the rest, but simply to *be* a minister, this will have to win its way slowly into Methodist minds and hearts. There will be suspicions that it will encourage laziness and colourless personalities and priestcraft. These must be countered in argument as they will certainly be proved false in experience. The advantage to be gained is a doctrine of the ministry which is rooted not only in the gifts which the Holy Spirit bestows and the authority which the Church confers but in the action of God in call and ordination to create (that is the best word) a man who shall represent him. In which case the answer to the question 'What *is* a minister?' is that he is a man of God.

REFERENCES

1 *South East Asia Journal of Theology*, vol. 4, no. 2. C. H. Hwang. October 1962. (Extract in *Patterns of Ministry*, p. 12 f, World Council of Churches, July 1965.)
2 *Christ, the Holy Spirit and the Ministry*, p. 11. World Council of Churches Study Booklet. May 1965.
3 *Who do they think we are?* Basil Moss, Parish and People. December 1964.
4 *Christ, the Holy Spirit and the Ministry*, p. 32. World Council of Churches Study Booklet. May 1965.
5 'Christ and the Church.' North American Section of the Report of the Theological Commission of the World Council of Churches. Quoted in *Laity*, p. 5. May 1963.
6 Statement of the Second Consultation on Theological Education in South East Asia (Hong Kong 1965). World Council of Churches, July 1965.
7 *Christ's Ministry through his whole Church and its Ministry*. World Council of Churches. Quoted in *Laity*, p. 16. May 1963.
8 *Christ, the Holy Spirit and the Ministry*, p. 17. World Council of Churches.
9 *The Protestant Ministry*. Daniel Jenkins. Faber and Faber, 1958.
10 *The Pioneer Ministry*, p. 60. Anthony Hanson. SCM Press, 1961.
11 Ibid., p. 62.
12 Ibid., p. 72.
13 Ibid., p. 157.
14 *The Doctrine of the Christian Ministry*, p. 127. John Line, Lutterworth, 1959.
15 *The Special Function and Responsibility of the Ordained Ministry*, (Patterns of Ministry in Europe Today). World Council of Churches, November 1965.
16 *Methodist Deed of Union*, clause 30.
17 *The Doctrine of the Christian Ministry*, p. 138. John Line. Lutterworth, 1959.

18 *Letters and Papers from Prison* (Second Edition, revised), p. 180. Dietrich Bonhoeffer. SCM Press, 1956.
19 *The Pioneer Ministry*, p. 157. Anthony Hanson. SCM Press, 1961.
20 Statement on 'Ordination in the Methodist Church'. Minutes of the Methodist Conference 1960, p. 241. Epworth Press.
21 'The Shape of the Ministry.' Report of the Working Party of the British Council of Churches, 1965.
22 *Institutes*, IV, 3, 1. John Calvin (translated by Henry Beveridge). James Clarke, 1957.
23 *The Theology of Calvin*, p. 201. Wilhelm Niesel. Lutterworth, 1956.
24 Ibid., p. 202.
25 *Institutes*, IV, 3, 1. John Calvin (translated by Henry Beveridge). James Clarke, 1957.
26 Ibid., IV, 3. 1.
27 *Corpus Reformatorum* 27.688. Quoted by Niesel. *The Theology of Calvin*, p. 203. Wilhelm Niesel. Lutterworth, 1956.
28 *Honest Religion for Secular Man*, p. 62. Lesslie Newbigin, SCM Press, 1966.
29 'The Ecclesiological Basis of the Plenitude of the Church: The Unity of Laity and Clergy in the Orthodox Tradition.' Nikos Nissiotis, in *Verbum Caro*, nos. 1-2, 1965. (Extract in *Patterns of Ministry*, p. 13 f. World Council of Churches, July 1965).
30 *Christ, the Holy Spirit and the Ministry*, p. 11. World Council of Churches, May 1965.
31 'Christ and the Church.' North American Section of the Report of the Theological Commission of the World Council of Churches. Quoted in *Laity*, p. 21, May 1963.
32 *The Doctrine of the Christian Ministry*, p. 129. John Line. Lutterworth, 1959.
33 Statement on 'Ordination in the Methodist Church'. Minutes of the Methodist Conference 1960, p. 240. Epworth Press.
34 *The Doctrine of the Christian Ministry*, p. 134. John Line. Lutterworth, 1959.
35 *Expository Times*, vol. LXXV, No 9, p. 265. David Stacey. T. & T. Clark, June 1964.
36 Report of the Third World Conference on Faith and Order (Lund, 1952). SCM Press, 1953.
37 *The Doctrine of the Christian Ministry*, p. 51. John Line. Lutterworth, 1959.
38 Ibid. p. 55.

39 *The Gospel according to St John*, p. 473. C. K. Barrett. SPCK, 1955.
40 Minutes of the Methodist Conference 1960, p. 235.
41 Statement on 'Ordination in the Methodist Church'. Minutes of the Methodist Conference 1960, p. 241.
42 Ibid., p. 241.
43 Minutes of the Methodist Conference 1960, p. 240.
44 Statement on 'Ordination in the Methodist Church'. Minutes of the Methodist Conference 1960, p. 241.

CHAPTER III

THE MINISTRY TODAY

THE theology of the ministry worked out in the preceding chapter cannot be left in a theoretical state. Some attempt must be made to see whether it makes any difference in practice. If we accept that a minister is not only the recipient of the Holy Spirit's gifts and the performer of authorized functions on behalf of the people of God but also a sacramental person, a man of God, who is different because he *is* what he *is*, just what difference does it make to his ministry? And is it conceivable that here we can find at least a partial answer to the confusions and frustrations that we had to record in the first chapter?

To believe that the ministry is an *ordo* created by God to represent him in the Church and the world is to set the minister's feet upon a rock. And that for two reasons. One concerns the old distinction between *being* and *doing*. In an age which has long since left medieval philosophy behind this must not be pressed too hard, but the two things are not the same. And if not, security is to be found in rocklike convictions about *being* rather than feverish activity in the realm of *doing*. This will not be readily acceptable to a generation that thinks empirically and sees so much value in active involvement. The attitude of the common man both to Christ and to Christians is indicative of this. The compassionate works of Christ are more meaningful to him than the doctrine of the Incarnation and the disinterested service of Christians in the community can make an impression where a theological position cannot. Nor will it be acceptable to the behaviourist who believes that the only valid conclusions that can be reached about human beings are all concerned with what they do. To him metaphysical concepts have no substance.

It will be obvious by now that our philosophy differs from his, though our respect for his point of view must make us consider presently the importance of what the minister does.

Again, some radical theologians will certainly regard our approach as repeating the folly of Lot's wife. Cornelis A. van Pewson, we are told by Harvey Cox in *The Secular City*, believes that we are now in a period of transition from what he calls the 'ontological' to what he calls the 'functional' periods of human history.[1] He disapproves of 'ontological thinking'. Harvey Cox himself believes that ontology and metaphysics are out of fashion and this may indeed be true. But the fact that common men, philosophers, and radical theologians find our view difficult to accept, however, does not mean that it is not true. We believe that to be sure of what you *are* is of more moment than being sure of what you *do* and gives a greater security. Acceptance of the doctrine that a minister is a man of God in the sense here described gives just that assurance.

The other reason why there is a deep certainty for the minister in this doctrine is that in it he has the assurance of both inward, subjective experience, and outward, objective fact, and both are necessary if he is to know that his feet are set upon a rock. On the subjective side he has the experience of his call, the 'pressure' put upon him by God which he knew in the secret place. He has too the experiential side of his ordination—the deeply moving effect of prayers said for him and hands laid upon him, the commitment of himself in the ordination vows. These experiences are not merely nostalgic memories, they are 'recalled' to him by the Holy Spirit at work within him and so are the means of deepening his faith and increasing his obedience.

But the necessary complement to this is the solid conviction that is anchored in objective facts. We suggested (page 53) that a minister ought to be conceived as different because he has been involved in certain *events* and we went on to show that in these events there is the making of a minister. It is in the constant 'recall' of these events—with all that they mean—under the stimulus of the Holy Spirit that assurance is to be found. As congregations will have heard in many a sermon, when Martin Luther was in a mood of depression and assailed by the devil he repeated to himself, 'I have been baptized'. He found inspiration in the event. The minister who is preyed upon by the various demons described in Chapter I, can fight back by first saying, 'I have been called'. Although the call came inwardly, the Church, after the most stringent tests, ratified it as a genuine call from God and so lifted it from the realm of the purely subjective. It is something that has happened and neither a perverse Invitation Committee nor an excess of demythologizing can change it.

Ordination demonstrates this truth incontrovertibly. It is conceivable—though highly unlikely—that both the candidate for the ministry and the Church were wrong and that in fact God did not call the man at all. But there is no disputing the reality of ordination. On a date and in a place that can be quoted, the prayers were said, the Holy Spirit was given through the imposition of hands, the commission and the authority were bestowed, the vows were made and the candidate was declared to be ordained. All this *happened*. God did, on that day, make a minister. That was an event, and therefore is unalterable. So the minister looks back in the spirit of Martin Luther and says, 'I have been ordained', and in the certainty of the sacramental event there is both security and comfort.

We can notice in passing that views of the ministry which we have rejected on other grounds are not able to give such a full assurance. The charismatic view, though it may provide subjective experiences, does not have the required association with objective events. The reality of the gift may not be in doubt but, because it is not anchored in a sacramental event, the ability of that gift to give assurance of the validity and efficacy of a whole ministry may very well be. Preaching is a case in point. Some ministers have the gift, and both they and the congregations who sit under them have enjoyed deep religious experiences as a result of it. But in these days when so many people put a question mark against every sermon that they hear and when it is no longer possible to fill or empty churches by preaching, the man whose ministry is primarily the exercise of this particular charismatic gift is liable to question his ministry.

The functional view of the ministry fails to give the required security because it is concerned with what a minister does rather than with what he is and it is about his functions and not his nature that all the modern questions are being asked. When people wonder what a minister is *for* they really mean that they see no relevance or importance in the things he does. And this is exactly what worries ministers themselves. Under the influence of radical theology and the pressures of an agnostic society they question whether preaching is able effectively to communicate the Gospel, whether sacraments are more than the esoteric rites of the favoured few and whether pastoral visitation does anything to advance the Kingdom of God. As illustrative of this, here are the comments on pastoral work of one of the more radical of the post-war generation of Methodist ministers:

With more and more people working during the day, and watching TV in the evenings, visits on the old pastoral pattern become increasingly impossible. More basic than this is the quiet way in which the minister has become a sort of spiritual baby-minder; a professional carer for people, doing visits which other members of the congregation ought to be doing (and would do if he were removed and no replacement made). Not to mince words, the minister is often little more than a church attendance officer, the servant of the congregation in a sense totally different and more degrading than being the servant of all in Christ's name means.

Criticisms, generally less sweeping than this, but still pointed, could be quoted of the relevance of preaching, sacramental observance, evangelistic practices and all the traditional ways of building up the life of the Church. In other words it is the functions that men are authorized to perform on behalf of the whole people of God that are being called in question. It is the difficulty of being convinced that what a minister *does* is anything more than gentle agitation on the periphery of life that causes concern. The functions are under fire.

It is therefore gratifying to notice that, though our rejection of the 'functional' view and our acceptance of a more 'catholic' one took place on theological grounds, on this more practical level the latter turns out to be the more propitious. For when the functions of the ministry are being written off by some and criticized by others, defended in their traditional form by some and modernized by others, it is an inestimable advantage if there is security and assurance for the minister concerning his ministry which rest on other foundations. This the present theology supplies. It turns from what a minister *does* to what he *is* by virtue of his call and ordination. He is, in all circumstances and whatever he is doing, the sacramental person, God's representative. And though he will try as hard as he can to exercise such charismatic gifts as he may have and to fulfil in the most relevant way the functions that he has been authorized to fulfil, his anchor is not here. It is the unalterable fact that God has created him a minister, and whatever state the Church or the world may be in, that is what *he is*.

At the same time it would be most unfortunate if this led to a lack of concern about the activity of the ministry today. To assert that the foundation of the ministry is 'ontological' is not to imply that the superstructure of its daily tasks is unimportant. On the contrary, having reached a firm conclusion about what a minister *is*, the inevitable question follows—what does a man who *is* this, *do*? Consequently the changes likely to emerge from modern criticism of the traditional patterns of ministry must not go unnoticed.

Preaching may come to mean snappy, racy dialogue instead of twenty-five minutes' worth of weighty exegesis; the Eucharist may become the Sunday morning family meal to celebrate the Resurrection and Living Presence of the Lord instead of the hushed and solemn addendum for the specially pious; pastoral care may come to mean the activity of laymen in house groups rather than ministers calling in the afternoons; the Church may be more effectively built up by its members digging the gardens of Old Age Pensioners than watching the transparencies of the holiday on the Costa Brava. In addition, new structures of the Church may at last be on the way. The long hours spent by Methodist ministers attending committees at local, circuit, district and connexional level, sitting out the September Synod, writing names on class tickets by the hundred, observing innumerable Standing Orders, filling up outsize schedules, racking their brains over stewardship campaigns that are resisted and building schemes that run into debt—these may undergo a metamorphosis as new insights into the nature of the Church, and particularly of the place of the laity within it, give rise to new structures. In all this the ministry will be seeking to fulfil the traditional functions in new and effective ways. There will doubtless be failures and controversy and heart-burning all round, but in the new forms that are coming to birth the ministry will go on, and those who argue that there is no place for a separated ministry will, even on these empirical grounds, be seen to be false prophets. All such changes in a minister's 'doing' are of consuming interest to those of us who argue that the theological basis of the ministry lies elsewhere. The fact that we do not mistake the foundation for the superstructure does not mean an indifference to the precise nature of the latter.

It is imperative, as one argues for a more 'catholic' doctrine of the ministry, that the obvious pitfalls should be avoided. We have contended (page 53) that the medieval view of the *esse* of the ministry should be set aside in favour of a more conceptual approach and now as we concern ourselves with the working out of the theology in the life of the ministry, there are complementary dangers to evade. One is that of interpreting the difference of the ordained minister in terms of status. This has to be avoided at all costs, otherwise those who in their 'protestant' fervour are quick to produce their stories of arrogant Irish priests, medieval prelates and 'spiky' Anglo-Catholics will be confirmed in their position. It cannot be said often enough that the ministry was, and is at every ordination, created to continue the ministry of Christ. The only status the minister has, and all he should desire, is the status of the carpenter who was crucified. In him and through him is the continuing ministry of the Son of Man who came not to be served but to serve (Mark 10:45), and if he is to have insignia they must be the towel and the basin. The word *minister* means *servant,* and the minister, like the Church of which he is a part, is called for service. For this reason, going beyond the *charismata* and the functions to the *nature* of the ministry should produce not less humility and disinterested service, but more. If it does not, the fault is in fallible human nature and not in the doctrine which, properly understood, relates the ministry more closely to Christ.

But there is a further danger. It is that in these days of theological and ethical turmoil, of confusion and doubt, a sacramental doctrine of the ministry will be escapist. Most things that are able to give security and comfort have this as a complementary danger. Hiding in the Rock of Ages can be an escape from reality and finding sanctuary in the Church can be a flight from the world. And one must face the prospect that when a minister discovers that his gifts are not producing the traditional results and the validity of his functions is constantly being questioned, he will retreat into the sacramental refuge, adopt a 'take it or leave it' attitude to the offer of the Gospel and sit back and preen himself on being the priestly man of God. But this is again to ignore the fact that the doctrine we are here advocating is that the ministry is given by God in order that the Incarnation may be carried on in every age.* It is the Son of Man who came 'to give his life a ransom for many' (Matthew 20:28b), who 'emptied himself, taking the form of a servant' (Philippians 2:7), who came 'to seek and to save that which was lost' (Luke 19:10), whose ministry is to be continued. And this ministry, from Baptism to Ascension, was not escapist. Though the danger of a 'high' doctrine of the ministry becoming escapist is real enough, it must be emphasized that this is a perversion of the doctrine and exactly the opposite of its intention.

To believe that the minister is a man of God in the sense here described is to give him security and assurance instead of frustration and confusion. Far from encouraging escapism, this is to serve as a firm, unshakeable base from which to launch into the exciting world of reappraisal and experiment which can increasingly be found in the Church of today. Knowing, as those who do not share his doctrine cannot, that the ministry resides in what he *is*, he is free to

---

* See pp. 62-3.

re-examine all the functions of ministry without the fear that if they are discovered to be irrelevant, or better done by somebody else, he will lose his *raison d'être*. We now enquire how this can be done. There are two ways in which the minister will proceed. One is to enquire whether his theology of the ministry can bring him to any new insights in the traditional, regular work of the ministry. The other is to ask whether it can lead him to an acceptance of those new patterns of ministry which are being so widely advocated today. We will take these in turn.

The first insight of this theology concerns the minister's piety. It would be quite improper to suggest that those who hold other views of the nature of the ministry than that put forward here are less diligent in their prayers and quite absurd to think that their prayers are less effectual. Generations of good and godly Methodist ministers who have believed in what, for want of better terms, we have described as the 'charismatic' and 'functional' views of the ministry, have rooted and grounded their ministry in their prayers. There must be no suggestion that the ontologist is more devout, but only that his different conception of the nature of the ministry may lead him to say his prayers differently.

In all probability they will be more liturgical* and the saying of a daily office will be compulsory. We noticed in the previous chapter that the conception of a sacramental person created through God's call and ordination is a move away from the more personal and subjective interpretation of the ministry. The emphasis is not upon the man as a man, but upon the man created to be the representative of God. Exercising gifts and fulfilling functions do in practice tend to bring into prominence the personal qualities and

* The word is here used in its popular rather than its literal sense.

abilities of the minister. This is, within limits, necessary and desirable and it is no part of our concern to argue against it, but only to insist that it is an inadequate conception of the ministry unless it is complemented by the view that what God creates through call and ordination is a minister, regardless (in that respect only) of the personal qualities and abilities of the man being acted upon. The brilliant preacher is no more *a minister* than his less lucid brother whose twenty minutes in the pulpit only bring him back to where he started.

It follows that the prayers likely to be used by the 'sacramental person' are those in which the personal, idiosyncratic element is less, that is, liturgical prayers. This is not to deny the regular and controlled use of free, extempore prayer in private devotions. It is to give such prayers their place within the ordered liturgy of a daily office, the bulk of which will be impersonal in the sense that it begins with God and the Gospel rather than the needs of the minister and such changes as occur in it are the result of the unfolding drama of our redemption in the Christian year and not of the mood and condition of the person at prayer.* The daily discipline which this imposes is not unacceptable to a conception of the ministry in which there is cool objectivity as well as a warmed heart.

If one section of the daily office is to be given any emphasis, it must be the Intercessions. The 'priestly' work for which the minister has been made is to represent God to man and man to God. The latter does not mean that he exercises a monopoly and that other men have no direct access to the Father. It means that systematically, and with deep concern, he acts as Intercessor, bringing his people and their needs into the holy place. He not only

---

* As judgements on liturgical offices are much better made from practice than theory a suggested daily office for Methodist ministers is included as an Appendix.

prays for them, he prays on their behalf, for they are too occupied to do it themselves. The country priest who rings the church bell before he says the appointed office is telling his people on the farms and in the fields that he is about to pray for them, and on their behalf. This is the work of the man of God.

The minister as Intercessor within the context of the daily office is representing man to God. The obverse side is the representation of God to man and here the insight afforded by this view of the ministry will concern the way in which the forgiveness of God is mediated to his people. Naturally there will be those who will contend vigorously that there is no need of mediation at all. 'There is one mediator between God and men,' they will quote, 'the man Christ Jesus' (I Timothy 2:5). To them it must be granted that the individual believer has unimpeded access to God to whom he can make his confession through Christ, and from whom he can receive his forgiveness, apprehending it through faith. Most Methodists have known nothing but this and one would not wish to question the reality of their experience. But two things must surely be conceded by them. One is that it is far too easy to kneel down and confess sins to God. The 'come-back' is, not invariably but very often, of the vaguest kind, so that what results is perilously near a dialogue with oneself. The effect of this is not so much a diminution of assurance—the believer has the firm, unshakeable promises of the Bible behind him— but a less thoroughgoing catharsis and an almost entire lack of that spiritual direction which has traditionally complemented the sacrament of penance in those churches that have it. The other concession is that apart from the place of private prayer—and sometimes there—the giving and receiving of forgiveness in Methodist practice is not unmediated. It may occur through reading the Bible, saying prayers in church, hearing the lessons being read or listening to the sermon. The question now before us is whether it can, and ought regularly, to occur through the mediation of the sacramental person. Or, not to offend I Timothy 2:5, through the mediation of Christ in which, by being what he is, the sacramental person has a share.

One of the numerous debts which the Church owes to the Taizé Community is the re-examination of confession and absolution and their reinstatement on a sound Reformed and Protestant basis. Max Thurian, in his excellent book on the subject, starts from the position that 'the sixteenth century Reformers, and after them the Lutheran and Reformed Churches, asserted that the practice of confession was both well-founded and profitable.'[2] Both Luther and Calvin were at pains to avoid non-biblical conceptions of contrition and penance, but both saw the value to the struggling Christian of what Calvin describes in the following sentences:

For it sometimes happens, that he who hears the general promises of God, which are addressed to the whole Church, nevertheless remains in some suspense, and is still disquieted with doubts as to the forgiveness of his sins. But if he discloses secretly to his Pastor his distress, and hears the Pastor applying to him in particular the general doctrine, he will be straightly assured where formerly he was in doubt, and will be liberated from every trepidation and find repose of conscience.[3]

One or two of the points made by Max Thurian ought to be noted. He puts cogently the argument for auricular confession:

It is easy to admit one's sin to someone whom one knows to be fully aware of it already. There is also the fact that we too easily become accustomed to the idea of the presence and holiness of God. The presence of a witness on behalf of God and of the Church makes more concrete for us the fact that God is there, that he is listening, grieving, and forgiving. The confessor, as a sign of the presence and the holiness of God, imparts to our confession a quality of committal and surrender which is an aid to humility. Furthermore, the presence of the confessor makes it possible for us to hear the liberating words of absolution.[4]

He argues for absolution on the only acceptable ground—that Christ absolved men during his ministry and that power of absolution must be a feature of any ministry which continues his. He emphasizes the value of spiritual direction. 'Director and directed together seek, in prayer and obedience to God's Word, the leading of the Holy Spirit.'[5] He insists quite properly on the centrality of Christ in the whole operation. The minister does nothing of himself, he does not presume upon 'his personal and spiritual authority or the exemplary character of his life in order to have the right to exercise his ministry'.... 'It is essential that the sole authority of Jesus Christ be recognized in the ministry of the confessor.'[6] It can be so recognized, we contend, because the minister is called and ordained precisely to that end.*

The relevant question is whether, if we are convinced that there is value in this, there is the slightest chance of it being practised by Methodist ministers. At first sight it would seem not. Confession is so universally associated with Roman Catholicism that it would be difficult in many places even to contemplate the possibility without hands being raised in holy, Protestant horror. But there are more rational objections. A Church which claims Assurance as one of 'our doctrines' and has its people singing:

> *O the rapturous height*
> *Of the holy delight*
> *Which I felt in the life-giving blood!*
> *Of my Saviour possessed*
> *I was perfectly blessed*
> *As if filled with the fullness of God,*

* The order of Confession used at Taizé is given as an Appendix so that the liturgical expression of these truths can be examined. Particular notice should be taken of the entire absence of sacerdotalism.

is not likely to be the first to see the need for the sacramental word of absolution. Again, Methodist ministers live very close to their people; the reciprocal use of Christian names between the minister and the leading laymen is very common, and it can be questioned whether they have the necessary detachment. Then they are under no vow of secrecy and though pastoral wisdom and personal integrity would usually be enough, a vow which is absolute would, for the penitent's comfort, be preferable. But undoubtedly, the main difficulty is the undefined feeling that sacramental confession lies outside of the Methodist ethos.

If the Methodist Church is to continue in isolation it is doubtful if any of this could be changed. Fortunately all the signs are that she is not. Closer relations and eventually union with other communions are bound to open the way for the consideration of practices which other Christians have found of immense spiritual value, and this might well be one. Certainly the politic way forward is not for ministers to try to persuade the laity to avail themselves of this means of grace. This would be rejected out of hand. The only possible way is for ministers, and particularly those whose theology is the theology of this book, to try this discipline for themselves and then let the results be their own advertisement. But even this will not be easy.

The mediatorial work of Christ through his ministers, expressed sacramentally in confession and absolution, is continued throughout the whole range of pastoral work. It is true, as we noticed in the first chapter, that the traditional pastoral methods have no effect on some, and they may well have to be changed. The pastoral prayer may come to be the exception rather than the rule and the conversation governed by a genuine concern in the total life of the people being visited may be the only acceptable medium—though this is not an excuse for failing to say the pastoral prayer when circumstances demand it. The encouraging point to be made here is that the pastoral situation is different when attention is turned from what a minister *does* to what he *is,* and the difference is more clearly seen when the person being visited, as well as the minister, accepts the view of the ministry for which we are contending. Once the people being visited believe that in their house is not only the affable man who is really interested in them, but the man of God, the sacramental person who is Christ's respresentative, then the possibility of fruitful pastoral work is not far away. Obviously in this secular age people are not going to fall over themselves to unburden their souls when the minister calls, and if the slightest suggestion of a pose is evident then the minister would have done better writing out class tickets at home. But surely the theology of the ministry such as we have outlined is now the *sine qua non* of any progress towards the re-establishment of a true pastoral relationship of a kind that can restore a sense of purpose to the faithful minister who spends so much time and travail in the regular visitation of his flock. Christ will continue to exercise his pastoral ministry through him, if both he and his people recognize that that is what he is *for.*

What insight can this theology bring to the traditional ministry of the Word and Sacraments? There will be a tendency for a 'sacramental person' to have a 'sacramental' ministry. The man who sees his ministry as rooted in objective events in which he has been involved will tend to see it working out in similar terms. The God who has *created* a minister in the sacramental act of ordination will be further seen as the God who in Baptism *creates* members of his Church and who in the Eucharist *creates* new men in Christ. The man who gives a 'high' meaning to the laying-on of hands will give a 'high' meaning to water and to bread and wine. They will be to him the signs infallible of the presence and activity of God. And the fact that his doctrine of the ministry means not primarily that he is the Reverend A. B. exercising certain gifts or performing specific functions but rather the Reverend A. B. *representing Christ* will draw him to the sacraments where the character and personality of the celebrant or administrator matter less than in other spheres.

This will be both to his advantage and to his disadvantage. In his own spiritual life he will be immensely strengthened, for the Eucharist will come to be for him an inexhaustible store of grace. The Table will be the place where he offers the oblation of his ministry, begs and receives his forgiveness, and encounters the living, reigning Lord whose man he is. It will enable him to continue in his ministry with conviction when without it he would be tempted to resign. The disadvantage is that he will not, within the general practice of Methodism, be able to communicate as often as his spiritual life demands and that attempts to remedy this are likely to meet with opposition from those who see any increase in sacramental observance as an un-Methodist attempt to ape the Anglicans. He can only press on with diplomacy and courage!

His corresponding temptation will be to place less emphasis upon preaching, and this is a temptation to be resisted. The Word and Sacraments must be held together, both having an equal and commanding importance. Whenever the Church has emphasized one to the exclusion of the other she has been the poorer for it and it has been the burden of the Liturgical Movement in our time to give them both their rightful place. The 'sacramental person' therefore will not allow his belief in and devotion to the sacraments to detract from the fact that he is a preacher. The preaching will be of two main kinds, distinguished by Richard Niebuhr in *The Purpose of the Church and its Ministry*[7] as evangelical and pastoral. Evangelical preaching is the proclamation of the Gospel to the unbeliever.

Pastoral preaching is 'directed towards the instruction, the persuasion, the counselling of persons who are becoming members of the body of Christ and who are carrying on the mission of the Church'. In both types of preaching, but to a greater extent in the former than the latter, the minister will be aware of the immense problems raised by attempts to communicate the Gospel through words. He will therefore be intensely interested and actively involved in the experiments in communication which are taking place in the churches. Dialogue sermons, interviews, the use of visual aids, all will be grist to his mill.

But there is something of greater importance. We noticed in Chapter I (page 28) that the chief lack in modern preaching is the lack of authority, and the 'sacramental person', as we call him for want of a better term, can contribute to the remedy for this lack. He cannot of course produce slick and ready answers to all the problems raised by radical theology, but he can provide the authority which resides in him as the man of God and the representative of Christ. Here again, if the dangers of an inflated ego or an unpleasant clericalism are to be avoided, the preaching ministry must be conceived as the continuing preaching ministry of Christ through the men called and ordained by God to continue it. Their every passing utterance will not have on it the stamp of eternal truth, but as they expound the Word of God under the guidance of the Holy Spirit, and so fulfil one of the purposes for which God made them ministers, they will be continuing the preaching ministry of the one who 'spoke with authority and not as the scribes'.

To believe this leads us to the 'high' view of preaching held by John Line who, after mentioning the preacher's 'thrusts and retreats in preparing a sermon', asks—and by implication answers—the question: 'If that (the thrusts and retreats) is convertible into the Word of God, does it not imply supernatural working as truly as anything priesthood may effect at Eucharist or Mass?'[8]

These then are the insights which this theology can bring to the traditional, regular work of the ministry. It will be self-evident that this position cannot in any circumstances be reconciled with that which argues for the abolition of the separated, ordained ministry—the 'we are all laymen now' school. For us, this is to reject one of God's greatest gifts to his Church. On the contrary, the doctrine that through call and ordination God created an *ordo* of men to be his representatives rediscovers the glory that is proper to the ministry and brings a much needed sense of purpose into its work. It is the fashion to denigrate the traditional, regular, routine work of the ministry, but this theology insists that when the minister is seen to be what he truly is it takes on a new meaning and significance. The regular circuit minister, therefore, holding this 'catholic' view will consider with humility the accusations that he is 'not socially relevant', 'only a paid secretary', 'wasting his time on useless structures', 'not doing a man-sized job' and so forth, but he will not be shaken by them, for he knows that *because he is what he is,* his feet are set upon a rock.

Not unnaturally this view will be regarded by some as a retreat into the old ways of the past when, as they think, the only hope for the ministry is an advance into the new ways of the future. This under-estimates the centrality and depth of the doctrine of the ministry with which we are concerned. The truth is that, when the ministry is conceived of as an *ordo* of 'sacramental persons', a sure foundation is laid for all those experiments in ministry which arise as more and more the Church comes to be seen not as an institution to be preserved by a professional class but as the servant of mankind whose ministers are there to serve. The theology of the ministry is of considerable importance for such experimental ministries. The point is made by

David Paton[9] when he notes that, apart from the Orthodox, the Friends and the Brethren (the last two have no separated ministry), it is the Anglicans more than others who have developed the theory and practice of voluntary clergy. He then asks, 'Is it because there is in Anglicanism a sufficiently strong doctrine of the ministry as a sacramental reality to enable a priest still to be, in his own eyes and those of the congregation, "a real priest", in spite of the fact that he has a full-time secular job and has not had a full professional training?' We hope the answer to his question is in the affirmative. Puting the point in our terms, some of the difficulties in dealing with new patterns of ministry arise from the persistence of the functional view which tends to tie the ministry down to the performing of those functions which have been duly authorized by the people of God. The view that the *esse* of the ministry resides elsewhere—in the person of the minister rather than his activity—gives room for more flexibility. This we must now try to show.

There is in the Church today a growing emphasis placed on specialized ministries.* This, it is argued, is the only way for the ministry to be viable in a society which is becoming more and more specialist. As a German sociologist puts it, 'There seems to be no other way left of interpreting and giving meaning to any kind of work except by carrying it out in the context of a profession. The part-time or honorary position in the political community, in societies and associations is disappearing.'[10] If the work of the ministry is to be done at a standard which is not shamed by the standards of the secular world then there must be specialization. It can take place both within and without the 'norm' of the ministry.

---

* In a World Council of Churches Report of 1965, it is stated that out of forty-eight thousand ministers in sixty-five churches, at least 4,762 (roughly 10%) were engaged in full-time non-parochial ministries.

Within the normal life of the Methodist ministry a certain amount of specialization is possible. Men can concentrate on the work at which they excel (not necessarily the same as what they like)—youth work, catechetical instruction, healing groups are examples—provided the staff of a circuit can, in a limited sense, work as a team. This has, however, been criticized as leading to 'the diffusion of ministerial oversight and pastoral care.'[11] Ministers can and do engage in specialized work like industrial, prison, hospital, university and training college chaplaincies, which lie out of the normal round of church life. Then there are the housing societies which have been fostered by the Church in areas of need, Marriage Guidance counselling, the presentation of the Gospel on television and radio and through films and the invaluable social work of Methodist Missions. More and more these demand the maximum time and attention that the minister can give. Within the limits imposed by the demands of his 'regular' ministry the more specialized he can become the better.

The point is then reached when the demand for specialization becomes a demand that the minister should be separated from the 'normal' work of the ministry, and in Methodist parlance he is given 'permission to serve' with an external organization. These vary enormously, from university professorships to departments of the British Council of Churches, from the Churches' Television Centre to the Council of Christians and Jews. One does not need prophetic insight to see that this question is likely to become even more lively in the future than it has been in the past. For on the one hand, demands for full-time specialization are certain to increase, and particularly the demand that ministers should be granted permission to serve as teachers in the schools. In addition, if the kind of movement described in Colin Williams' *Where in the World?*[12] proves to be the emerging pattern, then there will be a shift in emphasis from parochial to specialized ministries. On the other hand, with the decreasing number of candidates there is likely to be a shortage of men for the 'regular' work of the ministry. Many arguments are likely to be waged between those who contend that specialization is the only way in which to do the job efficiently and those who assert that 'specialized ministries increase the atomization of man's life in modern society instead of demonstrating in the unity promised by Christ; they slip into an unthinking solidarity with the secular structures they are supposed to serve.'[13]

Our concern here is not with the politics of this situation but with its theology. It can be very quickly and simply stated. If the *esse* of the minister lies in what God has created him to be rather than in what the Church authorizes him to do, then there are no theological grounds for supposing that an ordained man teaching Latin in a grammar school is any less a minister than his colleague in the regular circuit ministry. Though the nature of the work done is obviously of importance—and permission is only granted where its value to the community is evident—the fact remains that in our theology a minister is a minister *whatever he does*. And if more specialization is to be the mark of the ministry in the future it is helpful to know that we have a sound theological basis for it.

This is also relevant to group or team ministries. According to information given to a Working Group of the World Council of Churches Division of Studies (November 1965), there are sixty-three group or team ministries in Great Britain involving some three hundred ministers of six churches. Four or five of these teams represent interdenominational co-operation. There is some confusion over the use of terms. In the Methodist Report on the 'Deployment of the Ministry'[14] a group ministry is exercised from one specific centre, a team ministry from a number of different centres. The World Council of Churches Working Party, and the Paul Report, use the terms the other way round. We are here thinking of the group ministry as Methodists understand it and as it is exemplified for them in the splendid work being done at Notting Hill. Thinking about ministerial functions has to be revised in this context. As one of the Notting Hill group says, there is 'a great deal of energy and time spent on social issues and political action . . . a volume of care and case work, of work camps, conferences and time spent with young people, which the typical Methodist Church would not have countenanced in its ministry.'[15] 'Much less time', he adds, 'must be spent on circuit work and committees and church functions.'

Two further points need briefly to be made concerning group ministry. One is that, though by no means a panacea for all ecclesiastical ills, it is likely to be used more and more. Encouraged and inspired by what has happened at Notting Hill, the more forward-looking ministers are likely to press for it and be eager to participate in it. The other is that there is, and must continue to be, a very considerable flexibility in what is done by the ministers in such a group. They never know what they may have to do next.

Again, we have the right theological basis for such a ministry. A charismatic basis, even if theologically adequate, would tend to produce the one type of minister whom it is impossible to have in a group ministry—the *prima donna* parson. A functional basis is inadequate where ministerial functions are freely shared and where some functions are performed which the average Methodist would not recognize as ministerial. On the other hand— leaving aside the whole question of the laity to which we shall presently come—a group of 'sacramental men' who are ministers *in themselves* can do anything and everything that the situation of the group demands, and do it *as ministers*. The man arguing with the Social Council about converting houses into flats is just as much the minister as the man celebrating Holy Communion, for both are ministers *in their persons*. This is an adequate theological basis for group ministry.

In the ferment of ideas about the ministry and its future one is constantly meeting suggestions for a 'tent-making' ministry. This can come about in two ways. Ordained ministers, trained in the traditional way, can, possibly after further specialist training, come out of the 'regular' work and do full-time secular jobs as 'worker-priests'. Or it can happen the other way round and laymen in secular jobs can, after suitable theological training, be ordained to the ministry without giving up their employment. Either way it is important that what is done should not be done as a salvage operation to rescue the ministry from the plight caused by the shortage of candidates, but out of conviction concerning both the mission of the Church and the nature of the ministry.

Bishop Lesslie Newbigin, from his belief in the missionary character of the Church, argues for 'the development of a non-professional ministry exercised by men who continued to fulfil their secular callings.'[16] This is applicable to the younger churches where small, poor and scattered congregations who cannot sustain a full-time professional minister of their own can have, through the ordination of new converts still in their normal occupations, the full ministry of the Church from the beginning. By such a step the local church can cease to be yet another 'place on the plan' (to use Methodist terminology) to be visited by an overworked missionary or his colleague, and become a centre for advance. 'The new congregations', says Bishop Newbigin, referring to South India, 'were acknowledged from the beginning as truly the Church of God, responsible to God for letting the light of Christ shine in their village and beyond.'[17] These ideas have not gone unquestioned,* but Bishop Newbigin speaks from first-hand experience.

It has been advocated that the same thing should be done in modern, urban societies. House churches have been suggested—and in some places instituted—in which the ordained minister, when his day's work in the factory is over, celebrates the Eucharist on the dining room table with his neighbours and workmates standing round. An example from Hong Kong of this type of ministry fulfilling the mission of the Church is worth quoting. It is written by Dr H. Boone Porter of New York.

> How do the auxiliary clergy of Hong Kong commend themselves to the laity, and to the unevangelized public? The present writer can only say that on a blisteringly hot Saturday afternoon he has stood on a hillock outside Kowloon and watched Chinese workmen struggling to dig out a level space of ground, picking, dragging and rolling aside great stones while perspiration poured from their bare muscular backs. They were clearing a little play-ground for a Christian orphanage. These men were not being paid; I was told that most of them were not Christians. Why then were they doing this work? The orphanage was operated by an auxiliary priest and his wife. This man was employed during the week as an official of the medical department of Hong Kong. The men who worked under him had such admiration and respect for what he was doing at the weekends that they had volunteered to give up their Saturday holiday to do this back-breaking work for his orphanage. Here I saw the leaven of Christ visibly working in the world.[18]

We must also take note of experiments that have been made the other way round—not of laymen becoming ministers and keeping their lay occupations—but of ministers taking up lay occupations. This is not the place to tell the story of the worker-priests in France nor to list the advantages and disadvantages of the method employed

* Can they, for example, provide an educated ministry so necessary in a society where the standards of education are continually rising? And is not this a departure from what Dr Justus Freytag (quoted on p. 91) is asking for?

both there and elsewhere. The movement has its own literature which is easily accessible.* It was born, in this as in other generations, out of a deep conviction that, as Canon Max Warren puts it, 'the Church is Mission', and in that conviction it continues to make its contribution. Its purpose, it need hardly be said, is not to bring the 'working class' back to Church, but to involve the Church in the secular world. To talk at length to a worker-priest (as the present writer was privileged to do both at Pontigny and at Southall) is to have one's faith in the Church and her mission re-kindled.

Numerous writers on the present and proposed experiments in ministry have pointed out that, necessary as these new patterns may come to be, some full-time theological and liturgical specialists will always be needed. So will other men who combine theology with the cure of souls. As Anthony Hanson puts it: 'For theology to flourish a class of people is necessary who are both thinking about the faith and engaged in pastoral care.'[19] The ordained who have secular jobs will have to live to a certain extent upon the theological and liturgical capital of those who have more time to give to their books. This division in the ministry is no new thing, for it reaches back to New Testament times when the 'tent-making' ministry and the full-time, financially-supported ministry quickly came to co-exist.†

* Gregor Siefer, *The Church and Industrial Society*; D. L. Edwards, (ed.), *Priests and Workers*; John Rowe, *Priests and Workers: A Rejoinder*.

† Professor André Dumas of the Reformed Church of France summarizes the New Testament position in a paper to a World Council of Churches working group: 'The New Testament permits a minister to work as a professional receiving his salary from the Church with a good conscience. It also permits him, for evangelical reasons, to take an occupation which is not paid by the Church in order to continue to serve a specific community which cannot or will not support him.'[20]

Our contention is that the unifying theological factor that binds together full-time professional clergy, the men in secular jobs who have been ordained and ministers who have entered secular employment is that, by virtue of their call and ordination, they are all ministers *in themselves*. The gifts they possess and the functions they fulfil are widely different. One man visits the sick while another tends a lathe. One man marks Hebrew papers while another grinds a machine tool. But if God has created them ministers, then wherever they are and whatever they are doing, that is what they are. When the nature of their ministry is safe-that may well prove to be invaluable to the Church in the guarded by this doctrine they have a freedom to experiment that may well prove to be invaluable to the Church in the future as she seeks to fulfil her mission to the world.

The theme of this book, that the answer to the predicament of the ministry is in a 'high' understanding of the nature of the ministry is, at first sight, in opposition to much that is being said and written on the subject today. The current emphasis is on the fact that the ministry is the ministry of the whole Church and this, it is argued, means the virtual elimination of any difference between minister and layman. 'The dichotomy between minister and layman had to go', said Dr Leslie Davison at the Methodist Conference of 1966. 'They were both together, the people of God.' Thinking of the ministry as different from the laity is retrograde because it destroys the wholeness of the people of God. 'However much we may discuss and practise lay leadership, by the fact of having a group of ordained men set apart from the rest we have a Church composed of first and second class citizens'—so writes the Rev. Raymond Billington in the *Methodist Recorder*.[21] The balance is being redressed by a never-ending flow of paperbacks, spelling out in this layman's age the theology of the laity for the layman's Church. The means of redressing is the insistence that the ministry and mission of the Church is that of the whole people of God and not of one class within it. In the 'layman's Church' the ordained minister becomes an equal partner in a common enterprise or a 'back-room boy' whose function is to equip the laity for fighting the real battles or he virtually disappears. We are all laymen now. In Billington's precise words, 'We are all laymen with different ministries to fulfil'.

With much of this we are in agreement. The ministry of the Church is essentially, both now and in New Testament times, a corporate activity. We would not wish to be associated with the view, so strongly rejected by Anthony Hanson,[22] that the ministry can exist without the Church. This is the danger in any 'catholic' doctrine of the ministry where the impression is sometimes given (Hanson cites the Lambeth Quadrilateral) that the Bible, the Creeds, the Sacraments and the Ministry could be preserved and perpetuated by the ministry alone. This is contrary to New Testament thought and practice, where ministry and Church are indissolubly joined, and the theology of the ministry we are advocating does not support it. A difference in *being* (and we have thought of it conceptually) does not mean an independent existence and an *ordo*, almost by definition, is a group existing within a larger group. Laity and ministry together make the Church. The people of God are indeed one people and their mission to the world is the mission of one people. In this the laity are of of immense importance and their partnership with the ministry so crucial that it is worth examining the precise nature of it.

We have already established that the *charismata* of ministry are freely shared between them (page 39). 'The Spirit divides his gifts severally as he wills.' The partnership between ministers and laity is a partnership in which wisdom, knowledge, faith, healing and prophecy, to mention only some of the gifts of I Corinthians 12, are shared. We have also established (pages 49-50) that many of the functions of ministry are shared between the ministry and the laity. Proclamation is one of them and it should be our concern that when a layman exercises it it should be recognized as the representative action of the people of God and not as a second-rate substitute for the parson. Pastoral care is another and we have to resist the idea that a visit from a layman with a class ticket is not really a 'church visit' at all. This is orthodox Methodism and has no need of substantiation. The need is to practise more fully and effectively the partnership which our doctrine and constitution give us.

The chief difficulty in doing this is the equation, so deplored by all the radicals, of the ordained ministry with the full-time professional cleric—what Bishop Robinson calls *the professional line*.[23] What creates a rift within the people of God is not that one man is ordained and another is not, but that one is a professional and the other an amateur and the unfortunate equation of the ordained with the professional and the layman with the amateur. Nothing, so we are told, is more disruptive of the fellowship than this and nothing makes the mission of the one people of God so difficult to fulfil. The World Council of Churches' submission to the World Conference on Faith and Order at Montreal in 1963 declared, 'Each ordination for an office which at the same time becomes an occupation tends to set apart and isolate from, instead of becoming a commission within and for, the people.' W. G. Symons, a factory inspector from Birkenhead, writing in *Laity*,[24] makes the same point more strongly.

In the course of history, certain church offices have become 'full-time professions' and that fact has an immense influence on the self-consciousness of those who fill those offices; it calls into play all the powerful forces of group-consciousness, vested interest, the necessities of professional discipline and so on. This fact of ministerial professionalism is often more potent than theories or ordination in determining the relations between ministers and laity.

How can there be true partnership where this atmosphere exists? If the ministry of the Church is to be the one ministry of the people of God and the partnership between ministers and laity to be the fruitful thing it can be, then the equation of ordained ministry with full-time professional ministry will have to disappear. It is just because some of the proposed new patterns for the ministry aim to do this that they are so promising for the future of the Church.

In the establishment of this partnership another notion has to be set aside. One of the results of the emphasis on 'the layman's church' was the contention by some writers that the purpose of the ministry was to provide the theological expertise which the laity needed as they went out to fulfil the mission of the Church in the world. That somebody has to provide such expertise is true, for theology can only be understood and interpreted by theologians. It is the assumption that this is the function of the entire ordained ministry that is wrong. Providing expertise is the function of the expert. The expert needs to be a full-time professional. But it is not necessarily true that in the Church of the future the full-time professionals will be, as they are now, the ordained ministry. Indeed, real partnership between ministry and laity demands that they should not be.

Once we have rejected the professional-amateur, full-time-part-time distinctions between ministry and laity as undesirable, the way is open to describe the real distinction upon which alone a true partnership can be built. This distinction is partly functional in so far as traditionally ordination confers upon the ordained authority to perform certain functions, particularly that of celebrating the Eucharist. But primarily the distinction is not functional but sacramental. To reiterate, a minister is, through call and ordination, made a sacramental person and in this resides his difference from a layman. No doubt by now the critic will want to know precisely what is meant by this. He will ask just how, having set charismatic and functional differences aside, a minister is a different representative of God from a layman. What difference does being a sacramental person really make?

The question is similar to the one that demands to know what is the point of bread and wine when quite plainly God can be known and experienced without them. It is also similar to the question that asks what is the point of baptizing a child when, if God is love, it is obvious that he will not reject the unbaptized on the grounds of their deficiency. And the answers follow two lines of thought. One is that God constantly acts through what he has created. In the most materialistic of all religions it is water and bread and wine that he uses. *And people.* Supremely indeed, one Person. The other is that though we cannot limit the sphere of God's activity he does appear to particularize, to use the method of selection. Out of many nations he chose Israel, and it all narrowed down, as C. S. Lewis once said, to a Jewish maiden saying her prayers. Out of all the heathen he chose the Church, 'called to be saints'. Out of the entire physical world he chose for his Church water and bread and wine. Out of his Church he chooses and calls the ministry. They are the sacramental people, just as the bread and wine are the sacramental food. Nobody dare say that God cannot work through others (who are often better Christians) as well as through them, just as nobody dare say that God cannot forgive and restore and bless through a sermon or a prayer-meeting as well as through a Communion. But to question the existence of sacramental persons is to question the way that God has chosen to order his affairs with men. Once this is recognized the theological basis for a true partnership between ministers and laity is established, and all notions of professional and amateur, superior and inferior, competent and incompetent and the rest disappear into the limbo where they properly belong. In the partnership of the ordained and the baptized one is not 'higher' than the other, for it is a partnership in love. But, in the economy of God, they are *different* from one another.

From the Methodist ministry as we conceive it there is no escape. The nature of resignation depends upon what the ministry is believed to be. If it is conceived in terms of exercising gifts or fulfilling functions then resignation means that, regrettably, the conclusion has been reached that the gifts can no longer be exercised nor the functions fulfilled with a good conscience. The Church then responds by, in effect, withdrawing its authorization and the man is no longer appointed to a circuit, no longer 'planned' to preach the Word and celebrate the Sacraments. This is always a sad, and often a tragic, event, but on a charismatic or functional view of the ministry it is at least possible. On our view it is not possible. To be precise, it is obviously possible to 'resign from the ministry' in the sense of not engaging in the active work. What is not possible is to resign from *being a minister*. One may just as well try to undo one's baptism. The water will simply not come off. What God has done in his creative, sacramental activity cannot be undone. 'Once a minister, always a minister' is the only theology that can do God justice. It is this truth surely that the Methodist Church is accepting when it insists that if Methodist ministers resign, their orders are not lost but 'in suspension' and when it refuses to 're-ordain' (a meaningless word!) them on return. Once we are made ministers we are made for life.

This is the truth we have to contemplate when we are faced with the confusions and frustrations described earlier in this book. As men come into the middle years of the ministry one or other of these, or more likely a combination of several, assail them and the possibility of resignation may well present itself to their minds. This is the moment when theology counts. If it is a question of exercising one's gifts in a different context (the probation service instead of the ministry) or of fulfilling other functions of ministry (teaching backward children instead of speaking at the Women's Meeting) then the transition can be effected, the particular frustration relieved, and doubts entertained about the truth of the Gospel will not give rise to a guilty conscience. The minister becomes a layman again. But if our theology is right, and a minister is, through call and ordination, the creation of God, then this is simply not an option. *It is impossible for a minister to become a layman again.*

This can evoke two reactions. We can rail against God for what he has done to us. We can protest to high heaven that it is a monstrous injustice that our freedom should so be taken away. And no doubt notice will be taken of our imprecations. Or we can do what the saints have always done, and recognize that to be a slave in the service of God is better than to be a free man outside it. Ordained ministers are the slaves of God, and there is no escape. Nor, in spite of all the confusions and frustrations, do we seek any. To believe such a theology, and to see one's life in terms of it, requires (if one may say so without offence to people who don't believe it) not so much intellectual assent, as grace. Fortunately grace is the one thing of which there is an unlimited supply.

It would make an impressive ending to this book if it could be cogently argued that to believe and preach this doctrine of the ministry would bring the candidates for the ministry rolling back again. It might, if they saw its high sacramental character and its irrevocability as a totalitarian demand to which they must respond. But it might not, and there is evidence that all is not well, in this country at least, with the supply of candidates for the Anglican and Roman priesthoods. The only reason for proclaiming our theology is that we believe it to be true. The effect on those whom God will call into his ministry remains to be seen.

REFERENCES

1 *The Secular City*. Harvey E. Cox. SCM Press, 1965.
2 *Confession*, p. 22. Max Thurian. SCM Press, 1958.
3 *Institutes*, III, 4, 14. Quoted by Max Thurian, pp. 37-8.
4 *Confession*, p. 74. Max Thurian. SCM Press, 1958.
5 Ibid., p. 70.
6 Ibid., p. 101.
7 *The Purpose of the Church and its Ministry*. Richard Niebuhr. Harper Bros., 1956.
8 *The Doctrine of the Christian Ministry*, p. 154. John Line. Lutterworth, 1959.
9 *New Forms of Ministry*, p. 12. Ed., David Paton. Edinburgh House Press, 1965.
10 'The Ministry as a Profession: A Sociological Critique.' Justus Freytag, in *New Forms of Ministry*, ed. David Paton. Edinburgh House Press, 1965.
11 Policy Paper No. 1, p. 3. Methodist Renewal Group.
12 *Where in the World?* Colin Williams. Epworth Press, 1963.
13 *Kirchliche Experimente in Westdeutschland. Concept. Deutsches Heft* III, Winter 1963-4. (Quoted in *Patterns of Ministry in Europe Today*, p. 14. World Council of Churches, November 1965.)
14 Methodist Report on 'Deployment of the Ministry'.
15 *New Directions*. Norwyn Denny. December 1964.
16 *Honest Religion for Secular Man*, p. 114. Lesslie Newbigin. SCM Press, 1966.
17 Ibid., p. 114.
18 'Modern Experience in Practice.' H. Boone Porter in *New Forms of Ministry*, ed. David Paton. Edinburgh House Press, 1965.

19 'Shepherd, Teacher and Celebrant in the New Testament Conception of the Ministry'. Anthony Hanson in *New Forms of Ministry*, ed. David Paton. Edinburgh House Press, 1965.
20 'World Council of Churches Working Group Paper, The Pastoral Ministry considered as a Profession.' Professor André Dumas. *Patterns of Ministry in Europe Today*, p. 24. World Council of Churches, November 1965.
21 The *Methodist Recorder*, 7th April, 1966.
22 *The Pioneer Ministry*, p. 88. Anthony Hanson. SCM Press, 1961.
23 *The New Reformation?*, p. 57. John A. T. Robinson. SCM Press, 1965.
24 *Laity*, p. 44. W. G. Symons. World Council of Churches, May 1963.

APPENDIX I

A SUGGESTED DAILY OFFICE FOR METHODIST MINISTERS

In the Name of the Father and of the Son and of the Holy Ghost. AMEN.

Open, O Lord, my lips to praise Thy Holy Name: cleanse also my heart from vain, evil and wandering thoughts; enlighten my understanding, and kindle my affection; that I may be meet to be heard before the presence of Thy Divine Majesty; through Jesus Christ our Lord. AMEN.

> The Lord's Prayer
> The Psalm followed by *Gloria Patri*
> The Lection
> The Meditation
> The General Thanksgiving
> The Collect for the Day

For the Peace of the World
Almighty God, from whom all thoughts of truth and peace proceed: Kindle, we pray thee, in the hearts of all men the true love of peace; and guide with Thy pure and peaceable wisdom those who take counsel for the nations of the earth; that in tranquillity Thy kingdom may go forward, till the earth is filled with the knowledge of Thy love; through Jesus Christ our Lord. AMEN.

For the Unity of the Church
O Lord Jesus Christ, who didst say to Thine Apostles: Peace I leave with you, My peace I give unto you, regard not my sins but the faith of Thy Church, and grant her

peace and unity according to Thy will, Who livest and reignest, God, world without end. AMEN.

For the saints

O Lord our God, we praise Thee for the holy Apostles, Saints and Martyrs, and for all who have gone before us in the Faith and are now at rest. Grant that in the communion of saints we may become their true companions and with them keep Thy commandments unto the end. Through Jesus Christ our Lord. AMEN.

Pastoral and private Intercessions.

For Grace

O Lord our heavenly Father, Almighty and everlasting God, who hast safely brought us to the beginning of this day: Defend us in the same with Thy mighty power; and grant that this day we fall into no sin, neither run into any kind of danger; but that all our doings may be ordered by Thy governance, to do always that is righteous in Thy sight; through Jesus Christ our Lord. AMEN.

The Grace.

NOTES

1 The reason that there is no Confession in this office is that it is a Morning Office and it is assumed that confession will have been made the night before. It is not good to carry the sins of one day forward to the next.

2 The Wesley College Lectionary with the appropriate psalms is recommended. This lectionary gives a single daily reading for six days per week.

3 The Meditation should change weekly. Texts suitable to the season of the Christian year can soon be chosen.

4 The Collect for the Day can be taken from the Methodist Book of Offices in which case it will change weekly. Additional collects for use on Biblical Saints' Days are in the Book of Common Prayer.

APPENDIX II

CONFESSION AS PRACTISED IN THE TAIZE COMMUNITY*

BLESSING

Penitent: Brother, give me thy blessing.

Confessor: The Lord be in thy heart and on thy lips, that thou mayest truly confess all thy sins, in the Name of the Father, and of the Son, and of the Holy Ghost.   AMEN.

CONFESSION

Penitent: I confess to Almighty God, in the communion of saints in heaven and on earth, and before thee, brother, that I have sinned exceedingly in thought, word, and deed . . . (Here the penitent makes his confession, and then concludes:) It is my fault, my own fault, my own most grievous fault; wherefore I beg thee, brother, in the communion of the saints in heaven and on earth, to pray for me to the Lord our God.

(The confessor may ask such questions and make such exhortations as is necessary.)

ABSOLUTION

Confessor: Almighty God have mercy upon thee, and having forgiven thee thy sins bring thee to everlasting life.

* *Confession.* Max Thurian, pp. 138-9. By kind permission of S.C.M. Press.

Penitent: **Amen.**

(The confessor rises and stands in front of the penitent.)

Confessor: The Lord breathed on his disciples and said unto them, Receive ye the Holy Ghost: Whose soever sins ye remit, they are remitted unto them; and whose soever sins ye retain, they are retained.

(The confessor may lay his hands on the penitent.)

May our Lord Jesus Christ absolve thee: and I by His authority do absolve thee from every bond of sin.
Thus do I grant thee absolution from thy sins, in the Name of the Father, and of the Son, and of the Holy Ghost.

AMEN.

PRAYER

The Passion of our Lord Jesus Christ be for thee the only source of remission of sins, the increase of faith, and the reward of eternal life. AMEN.

DISMISSAL

Thy sins are forgiven; thy faith hath saved thee; go in peace!

APPENDIX III

POSSIBLE CHANGES IN THE METHODIST ORDINAL

Since the material in this book was prepared there has appeared the Interim Statement of the Anglican-Methodist Unity Commission *Towards Reconciliation*,[1] containing a new Draft Ordinal. The Ordinal is presented to the two churches as a proposal and it may subsequently be modified or even rejected. But supposing it is accepted, with only minor alterations, will it make any difference to the argument from the (present) Methodist Ordination Service in chapter 2 of this book? The answer is that it will not, as the following references show.[2]

(i) Prayer for those to be ordained. The primitive nature of this is referred to in the Introduction (pp. 51-2). At the moment of the laying-on of hands there is the prayer, 'Send thy Holy Spirit upon thy Servant N. whom thou hast called to be a Presbyter in thy Church'. In so far as this is petitionary it is more like the previous Methodist form than the previous Anglican one. A prayer for the gift of the Holy Spirit is also, as in the present Methodist service, embodied in a hymn. The *Veni Creator Spiritus* can be sung in either the version 'Come, O Creator Spirit, come' or 'Come Holy Ghost our souls inspire'.

(ii) The laying-on of hands. This of course is unchanged. The idea of commission is present in the bishop's prayer that follows. The ordained are now to be 'faithful and true pastors' who have 'sheep committed to their care'. They are to be 'apt and profitable fellow-workers with their brethren in the ministry'. The word 'dispenser' has gone but the bishop prays that the newly-ordained presbyters may 'proclaim effectually the Gospel of thy salvation' and 'minister the Sacraments of thy New Covenant', all in the apostolic tradition.

(iii) The giving of the Bible. In the Draft Ordinal the Bible is still given, and is described as 'a token of the authority which you have received from God to preach the Gospel of Christ and to minister the Sacraments of the New Covenant'. Our main contention that this *makes a difference* is unchanged.

(iv) Declaration of Ordination. Instead of the declaration by the President 'I hereby declare you to be ordained to the office of the Holy Ministry' in the Post-Communion Prayer God is asked to look graciously upon those 'whom thou hast made thy Ministers this day'. This makes more explicit our point that the creative activity of God is involved in Ordination.

(v) The Ordination vows. In 'The Examination', as it is now called, the questions asked are substantially the same as those in the present service. The total commitment, which makes the difference, is still there.

In brief, if the Draft Ordinal is accepted it will call for no change in the argument of this book; only the substitution of the new words for the old.

REFERENCES

1 Published SPCK and Epworth Press, 1967.
2 For the sake of brevity the references are from 'The Ordination of Presbyters, also called Priests', but the same points could be made from 'The Ordination of Deacons' and 'The Consecration of Bishops'.

www.ingramcontent.com/pod-product-compliance
Lightning Source LLC
Chambersburg PA
CBHW070508090426
42735CB00012B/2701